TIME MANAGEMENT
FOR THE
TIME-ANXIOUS

*A Guide to Managing Time for Those
Who Feel There's Never Enough*

SARAH BARRY

STORYLANE
BOOKS.

Edited by Suzanne Barry

Book Cover by Katarina Naskovski
Interior Layout by Nasir Ud Din Malik

Published by
Storylane Books
hello@storylanebooks.com
www.storylanebooks.com

TABLE OF CONTENTS

PREFACE

Do you ever hear the relentless ticking of the clock, even when it's silent? That's the echo of time anxiety—the insidious feeling that time is a predator, and we are its prey.

Time anxiety stealthily creeps into our lives, masquerading as the admirable pursuit of efficiency. But it turns the simple tick-tock that punctuates the passing of time into the heart-pounding drumbeat as the next deadline rushes forward and the battle must begin again. It's in the glance at your watch during a conversation or the misguided guilt when you pause to take that breath of fresh air, only to retreat—back into that pervasive realization that no amount of haste will ever see you catch up with the standards you have set for yourself.

Days, weeks, and months pass with boundaries blurred; each moment accounted for, already assigned to climbing over the mountain of tasks that stand between you and the completion of your goals. The joy of living in the "now" seems lost forever, subsumed in our panic to progress down our to-do lists, vision boards, and bucket lists. Life has become nothing more than a series of deadlines, milestones, and completions. Sound familiar? Of course, it does. I would know. I spent decades of my life rushing from deadline to deadline, punctuated by equally hectic vacations. And you? Well, you've picked up this title for a reason, so I know you can relate.

But there's hope yet. Let my years of time anxiety and my lessons learnt save you from your own missed opportunities and get you well on your way to living life in the moment. Don't worry. I didn't stop achieving my deadlines and completing my projects; in fact, my productivity improved—so did my relationships at work and home. I just learnt to enjoy the spaces in between deadlines using a series of strategies, attitudinal shifts, and a degree of self-education to better understand my internal and externalized processes around work. This is the purpose of this book—to share with you the multidisciplinary research conducted by a professional person who just wanted to enjoy her work life more.

Recognizing time anxiety is the first vital step towards untangling its tentacles and prying our well-being from its clutches. This is not a book about managing time; it's about managing the mind. It's about learning to slow the pulse of the day, to align with the rhythm in the chaos. Believe me, the rhythm it's there.

People have always juggled competing priorities—some of them quite life-threatening if we cast our minds back to prehistory and consider the immediate stress of survival. We have the tools to respond to modern stresses; we just have to understand ourselves, our processes and our relationship to time and pressure well enough to stay in control.

This is about redefining what it means to be productive—where success is measured not by how many tasks or meetings you crammed into your day, but rather how impactful you were in the meetings you scheduled, how attentive you were when your client or team briefed you on a situation, and how satisfied you felt by your present, engaged connection with your associates and projects.

By understanding your time anxiety responses, you take the first step toward liberating both your precious time from busywork and yourself from the grips of anxiety's wandering tentacles. I'm yet to hear anything other than this from anyone who has lived long and done it well: life is not about the moments you've raced through but those you've fully embraced.

CHAPTER 1

UNDERSTANDING TIME ANXIETY

E ver glance at the clock and feel your stomach drop, as if every tick is a countdown to an unmet obligation? You're grappling with time anxiety, a silent epidemic that's stealing peace from our every minute.

Part 1 Defining Time Anxiety: A Modern Epidemic

Time anxiety is not just about feeling a little stressed. It's that relentless pressure to sprint through tasks, coupled with the dread that you're never quite catching up. It's the beast that turns the gift of a 24-hour day into a never-ending treadmill of tasks. And it's rising—fueled by our digital age's promise of instantaneity, which leaves us, quite paradoxically, feeling even more crunched for time.

Image: Time anxiety will stay in hot pursuit, until you turn, face it, and take control!

Now, imagine a life where the clock doesn't mock you with its marching hands. A world where you don't measure your worth by how many items you've checked off your to-do list before lunch. Understanding and addressing time anxiety isn't just about finding more hours in the day—it's about changing the way we experience every hour. It's about transforming our approach from "racing against time" to "savoring the time we have." It's a paradigm shift from unconscious adherence to busy schedules, to purposeful decision-making about how we spend our moments and even how we feel about the moments as they pass us by.

Awareness is always the first step in any problem-solving venture, and conquering this modern epidemic is no different. Acknowledge that beast of time anxiety, learn its varied forms, and understand its impact, not only on your health and relationships, but also on your productivity. By recognizing the enemy, you begin the journey to reclaiming both your peace of mind and your control of the singular moments that make up your life.

Let's start a new narrative now. Let it be one where we control our schedules and not the other way around. Join the movement to dismantle time anxiety. This decision will be your first victory in the battle for a calmer, more fulfilling existence.

Part 2 Psychological Roots of Time Anxiety

The psychological roots of time anxiety are buried deep within our evolutionary history as a species, with variations and complexities arising from various cultural narratives that have always underpinned our social existence as humans. The base root of time anxiety is not merely a contemporary phenomenon but also a product of complex neurological and psychological processes that govern our perceptions and interactions with the world around us.

Historically, or should I say "prehistorically," (no matter our cultural background), our ancestors would have aligned their "rhythm of life" with the rhythms of nature. Governing periods of rest and activity through the rising and setting of the sun and the localized turning of the seasons, humans had no need to decide when to work and when to rest, or when to hunt and when to shelter, because nature decided that for them. That imprinting is millennia old, and it doesn't just drift away with the advent of time sheets and employment contracts that see us staring at blue screens way past our ancestors' bedtimes. The problem is that—without awareness—our internal rhythms will reach for an external timekeeper that nature once was, but the modern options are just not as healthy for us.

Prior to the Industrial Revolution, the majority of the population still roughly aligned with the rising and setting of the sun, with time marked using approximation and the occasional sundial. Trains arrived when they arrived, with station masters meeting lax schedules as best they could. People were generally more relaxed about time. With the Industrial Revolution came Greenwich time, uniform transport schedules, hours of work, and the rise of the clock as a central figure in human existence. Time became something to be measured, monitored, and managed. This shift lay the groundwork for the psychological relationship we now have with time—a relationship often characterized by anxiety.

One thing that does predate the Industrial Revolution is people's panic about dying before they have achieved their goals. History is full of leaders who accelerated their agendas as death neared, with sometimes chaotic results. This aspect of time anxiety can be traced back to an individual's desire for reputation and notoriety, or—in modern terms—just a sense that you haven't quite achieved what you expected at age 30, 40, or 50. Ever since Elliott Jaques coined the term "midlife crisis" in 1965, people have been aware they were having them, but as researcher and social commentator, Brené Brown, puts it, a midlife crisis is actually a midlife "unravelling." She says that it is actually just existence saying to you, "Time is growing short. There are unexplored adventures ahead of you." And there it is again . . . time anxiety.

So, time anxiety can stem from a fear of mortality—the ultimate deadline, but it can also be impending retirement, with unfulfilled promises made to your younger self. Each tick of the clock is a reminder of our finite existence, prompting us to question whether we are making the most of our limited time. This fear can propel us into a state of perpetual urgency, and the explanation is two-fold. On the one hand, we are compelled to speed through the remaining years, making up for lost time. On the other (less conscious) hand, some part of us feels that, by staying busy, we can fend off the inevitable.

So, yes, time anxiety is definitely about our relationship with ageing, the passing of time, and unmet aspirations, but another psychological phenomenon also contributes. Scarcity mindset theory tells us that humans place a higher value on resources perceived to be limited, and this plays a leading role in time anxiety. That same increased value placed on rare diamonds and waterfront properties is placed on time, as we watch it slip through our fingers. Time, undoubtedly finite, becomes a resource we feel we never have enough of, and this scarcity triggers anxiety. We become hyper-vigilant about wasting time, creating a paradoxical effect where we are so concerned with using time wisely that even when we do assign a few hours to pleasure, we can't enjoy it.

Perfectionism also feeds into time anxiety. The desire to make every moment count can create a pressure cooker of expectations. This is exacerbated in a society that lionizes hustle culture, equating busyness with importance and worth. The internalization of these values can lead to a relentless drive to optimize every second, reinforcing the anxiety loop.

Our digital age brings its own contributions. The constant barrage of information about what others are doing, often portrayed through the rose-tinted glasses of social media, can lead to social comparison and the fear of missing out (FOMO). This can compound time anxiety, as we worry that we're not living up to an ideal, or that time is slipping away without achieving the milestones that others seem to reach effortlessly.

Anxiety, at its core, is a manifestation of our response to perceived threats, and when time itself (or rather, its passing) becomes the threat, our cognitive and emotional resources are hijacked. The anticipatory anxiety about future events, combined with retrospective regret over a perception of an unproductive past, traps us in a temporal pincer movement that squeezes the joy out of the present moment.

Procrastination, often seen as a time management problem, can also be a symptom of deeper time anxiety. Task avoidance is sometimes a defense mechanism against the fear of failure or not meeting high standards within a set time frame. This can create a vicious cycle where procrastination leads to more time pressure, which in turn increases our anxiety as we feel ourselves struggling (and failing) to meet the targets we set for ourselves.

This is why the psychological roots of time anxiety are so deeply intertwined with our sense of identity and self-worth. Many feel that their productivity is an indicator of their value as a person. This self-imposed pressure can distort our time perception, making hours seem like minutes when we're under the gun and, conversely, making minutes seem like hours when we're waiting in anticipation or dreading an upcoming event.

To address the psychological roots of time anxiety, it's crucial to understand the multifaceted reasons behind it, from our evolutionary wiring and scarcity mindset to societal pressures and digital influences. With this understanding, we can begin to untangle the complex emotions tied to our experience of time and take steps to alleviate the anxiety associated with it. It involves cultivating a mindset that values presence over productivity, quality over quantity, and intrinsic satisfaction over external validation. By doing so, we can hope to redefine our relationship with time, transforming it from a source of anxiety to a space of opportunity and well-being.

Part 3 The Physiological Impact of Time Anxiety

The physiological impact of time anxiety is both pervasive and insidious, quietly infiltrating various aspects of our well-being. This form of anxiety goes beyond mere psychological discomfort—it manifests in the body, influencing everything from our nervous system to our immune response.

At the heart of the body's response to time anxiety is the stress response system, which has evolved over millennia to protect us from immediate physical harm. However, this system does not distinguish between physical and psychological threats, such as the pressure of a looming deadline or the chronic worry that we're not achieving enough daily. When time anxiety triggers the stress response, it sets off a cascade of hormonal changes, primarily the release of adrenaline and cortisol, preparing the body for "fight or flight."

Adrenaline increases heart rate, elevates blood pressure, and boosts energy supplies—useful in a physical confrontation or a sprint, but less so when we're sitting at our desks watching the clock. Cortisol, the primary stress hormone, alters immune system responses and suppresses the digestive, reproductive, and growth systems. In a chronic state of time anxiety, where cortisol levels are perpetually high, the body's normal reparative and restorative functions are disrupted. Essentially, our prehistoric body systems are responding to our schedule in a perfectly adaptive response to being chased by a tiger.

The problem is this: our physiological stress response is perfectly designed for a short, intense threat. One way or another, the stresses created by prehistoric events ended in a matter of moments. Our autonomic nervous system is simply not designed for prolonged stress responses. This constant state of high alert can lead to a multitude of physiological issues. Poor digestion, for example, may stem from the body prioritizing stress responses over normal digestive function. The immune system can become compromised, making us more susceptible to infections. High blood pressure and increased heart rate over prolonged periods put undue stress on the cardiovascular system, which can lead to heart disease or exacerbate existing conditions.

Likewise, time anxiety can lead to sleep disturbances. The anxious mind struggles to "switch off" at night, leading to difficulty falling asleep or staying asleep. Sleep is crucial for bodily repair and cognitive function; without it, we enter a vicious cycle where lack of sleep heightens anxiety, and anxiety further deteriorates sleep quality. We are trapped on high alert, our bodies convinced of imminent danger. But here's the thing, this "danger" message that sets our cortisol and adrenaline sky-rocketing comes from our own emotional reaction to time pressure—that is, how we *perceive* time sets off our fight-or-flight settings, not the situation itself.

All this constant stress is maladaptive for every single system in our bodies, including our muscles. Muscular tension is another common physiological manifestation of time anxiety. People may develop chronic neck, shoulder, or back pain due to the continual tension in these areas. In a perpetual state of preparedness for action, the body tightens muscles that rarely get the chance to relax. Over time, this tension can lead to issues like tension headaches, migraines, and musculoskeletal disorders.

The endocrine system, which regulates hormones, is also affected. Persistent stress can lead to insulin resistance and contribute to the development of type 2 diabetes, compounding the body's struggle to maintain balance.

Chronic time anxiety can also lead to long-term changes in the brain. The amygdala, the area responsible for emotional processing (and our fight-or-flight responses), can become hyperactive and hyper-reactive, making a person more sensitive to stress. Conversely, the hippocampus, which is critical for memory and learning, may become less active as the brain redirects resources toward dealing with the immediate perceived threat. Studies suggest that chronic stress can even lead to structural degeneration in the brain, impacting cognitive functions and memory.

The gut-brain axis—the bidirectional communication system between the central nervous system and the gut—can also be affected by time anxiety. Emerging research shows that chronic stress can alter gut bacteria, which can have widespread effects on overall health and mood, potentially contributing to the development of conditions like irritable bowel syndrome (IBS) or depression.

Time anxiety can lead to behavioral changes that further impact physiological health. Anxious individuals might turn to unhealthy coping mechanisms like overeating, smoking, or drinking, each with its own set of detrimental health effects.

The physiological impact of time anxiety is a clear reminder that our mental states are inextricably linked to our physical health. Time anxiety, left unchecked, can lead to a decline in overall well-being, making the management of this form of anxiety not just a psychological necessity but a physiological one as well. To counteract these effects, strategies to manage time anxiety and stress must be holistic, addressing both the mind and the body.

CHAPTER 2

THE PHILOSOPHY OF

TIME MANAGEMENT

Time management philosophy transcends schedules and checklists; it's about aligning one's values and priorities with how we spend the finite number of hours within each day. It's the art of making conscious decisions that reflect what truly matters to us, ensuring that our time is spent intentionally rather than reactively. Effective time management isn't just about efficiency; it's about creating space for reflection, rest, and connections that enrich our lives. It teaches us that by embracing our limits, we can focus our efforts on what we can control and, in doing so, create a life filled with purpose and presence.

Part 1 Shifting Paradigms: Time Quantity vs. Time Quality

In our fast-paced world, the quantity of time often overshadows its quality. The paradigm has long been to maximize every minute, squeezing as much as possible into the limited hours of the day. This approach measures time instead of output. Problematically, this relentless pursuit of productive moments fails to measure the effectiveness of the moments spent. This approach measures success by how full our calendars are, and not by the content of those appointments. The result? Days brimming with activity but devoid of meaning. The result? Accomplishment without fulfillment.

Shifting this paradigm is not just necessary; it's transformative. The concept of time quality brings into focus the richness of experience, the depth of engagement, and the satisfaction of being truly present. When we prioritize the quality of time, we savor the textures of our interactions, the nuances of our work, and the joy of moments that are not rushed but deeply lived. This doesn't mean we accomplish less; on the contrary, by concentrating on quality, we engage more fully, often leading to higher productivity and more profound achievements.

Quality time also reframes our mindset around leisure and rest. They are no longer gaps in productivity, but essential components of a well-rounded life. High-quality rest recharges the mind and soul, enhancing creativity and problem-solving when we do return to our tasks, refreshed and ready to re-engage. By appreciating—and, indeed ensuring—the quality of our non-working moments, we enrich the entire spectrum of our day-to-day existence.

Embracing time quality over quantity invites a more mindful approach to our lives. It challenges the notion that busyness is a badge of honor and replaces it with the understanding that true value lies in how we experience each moment. This doesn't just refer to how we "enjoy" each moment in a leisure sense, but also how satisfied we are with our creative output. Just as an elite athlete needs their ice bath as much as their gym workouts, our brains need that "time on ice" to regenerate. It's a paradigm shift that doesn't just change schedules; it changes lives.

Part 2 The Myth of "Catching Up"

The misconception that we just need to work harder and we will eventually "catch up" is endemic to the modern era. This illusion of temporal acceleration is an elusive goal chased by many, desperate to attain some semblance of peace and equilibrium. Anyone who has ever run through an airport or towards a bus stop to make up for a delay knows the next phase is recovery—as we stand gasping for air at the gate or bus stop. Our minds suffer the same burnout. The myth of catching up is just that, a myth. It's a misguided notion that can lead to a Sisyphean cycle of stress and unfulfillment.

The myth is predicated on the idea that there is a magical point at which all tasks are completed, all goals are met, and one can finally relax. It's the belief that time is a linear commodity that can be banked, saved, and retrieved; with enough speed and efficiency, one can outpace the relentless tick of the clock.

However, this concept fails to account for the nature of time itself and the reality of human capacity. Time is not something we can control; it flows continuously and impartially. Moreover, the list of potential tasks and responsibilities is infinite. New tasks will always arise, and goals evolve as we grow. If we view life in this manner, the finish line constantly moves forward as we chase it, creating an endless loop in which find ourselves trapped, and forever looking forward.

Image: Don't let the eternal 'to do list' rule your life. You choose what to do next!

The myth of catching up suggests that the present moment is merely a hurdle to overcome, rather than a space to inhabit and experience fully. It encourages a future-oriented mindset that can lead to a chronic state of procrastination and a habit of putting off life until a later date. But that "later" is a phantom, for as soon as one set of tasks is completed, another fills the void.

This falsehood also contributes to the devaluation of rest and recreation, making them feel like rewards that must be earned rather than necessary aspects of a balanced life. We postpone breaks until we're caught up, which means they often don't happen at all. This relentless pursuit can lead to burnout, a state of emotional, physical, and mental exhaustion caused by prolonged stress.

The myth of catching up is particularly pernicious because it ties our sense of worth and accomplishment to productivity. It fosters a culture where being busy is glorified, and downtime is often accompanied by a nagging sense of guilt. This approach is unsustainable and ignores the importance of restorative activities that rejuvenate our minds and bodies.

In reality, managing time effectively isn't about catching up but rather about setting realistic expectations and defining what is truly important. It's about recognizing that not all tasks are created equal and that saying "no" is often as powerful as ticking off items on a to-do list. Prioritization becomes key, and with it, the acceptance that some things may never get done—and that's okay.

It's also about understanding that time management is not an external system imposed upon us, but an internal approach to making choices that align with our values and enhance our well-being. True time management is about creating a life that reflects our priorities and allows us to savor the moments that matter most.

In dismantling the myth of catching up, we find liberation. We learn to live with the ebb and flow of life's demands, embracing productivity when it's needed and granting ourselves permission to pause. This shift in perspective transforms our relationship with time. The ticking clock shifts from adversary to ally, allowing us to find contentment and value in the present, even amidst the unfinished business of life.

Part 3 Time Perception: How We Experience Time

Time perception is a fascinating psychological phenomenon that refers to the subjective experience of time, which is influenced by various factors such as attention, memory, emotions, and the activities we engage in. Unlike the uniform ticking of a clock, our perception of time's passage can stretch and compress, wax and wane—making minutes feel like hours or hours feel like fleeting moments.

Our experience of time can be deeply psychological. When we are engrossed in an activity that captivates our attention, time appears to "fly." Conversely, when bored or waiting anxiously, time can seem to drag on forever. Equally interesting is how the years seem to pass more quickly as we age. A multiage New Year's Eve party might feature children impatiently waiting for the fireworks which are taking "literally forever!", while older guests wince at the thought of yet another year passing—exchanging disbelief at how the year has "simply whizzed by!"

This difference can actually be explained mathematically and is all about the fascinating concept of relativity. A year is only one seventh of a seven-year-old child's life, while the same year might represent one fiftieth of the life of one of their parents. It's the relationship between the year and the whole life span which determines how the passing of a year is perceived. This illustrates how our perception of time changes how we experience our lives at different times (and do different things).

This elasticity of time perception is known as the "relative" or "experienced" time, contrasting with the "absolute" time measured by clocks and calendars. And if that wasn't evidence enough, speak to someone who has completed Vipassana, a 10-day completely silent and still meditation course. They will tell you how their perception of time, and how one should spend it is, in some small way, forever altered. (Hint: Unstructured time is vital for true well-being and focus.)

This is not surprising because neurologically-speaking, the brain does not have a single, centralized "clock" but relies on a distributed system for perceiving time. This involves various brain regions, including the cerebellum, basal ganglia, and prefrontal cortex. Interestingly, the loop of activity between these three centers of the brain are also linked to focused attention, with deficiencies in this linked to attention issues, both clinical, such as with ADHD but also with subclinical behavioral tendencies. For example, dysregulation of the loop of activity between the cerebellum, basal ganglia, and prefrontal cortex can contribute to both attention deficits and impaired time perception. The intention to be on time may be present, but the person frequently underestimates the passage of time, earning the reputation for being chronically late and disorganized—or worse, not caring.

It's not fully understood how these components interact to produce our sense of temporal flow, but one thing is clear. Our time perception is an active brain construction, not a passive reception of external reality. Emotions play a crucial role in time perception. High arousal states, such as fear or excitement, can alter our sense of time. For example, during a frightening experience, it may seem like events are happening in slow motion. This could be because heightened emotional states trigger the brain to increase the resolution of perception, taking in more information per unit of time, and retrospectively, the event seems to have taken longer.

This is interesting because psychology research and theory links the retention of primal reflexes with attention disorders, and all of these emotions and primal reflexes happen in the ancient part of our brain. Our cerebellum has been saving us from tigers for millennia, while the cerebral cortex grew on top of this section of our brains as humans evolved.

Memory also significantly influences time perception. The more memory we have of an event, the longer it seems to have lasted. Remember the seven-year-old child at the New Year's Eve party? This is why new experiences, which require more processing and create more memories, can feel longer in hindsight. This phenomenon also explains why time seems to speed up as we age—familiar routines don't create as many new memories, and therefore, time appears to pass more quickly. For a child, life is unfamiliar. As we age, things get a bit more mundane and time speeds up.

Cultural factors can also influence how we perceive time. Different cultures have different orientations to time, often called "time culture." Some cultures are more "monochronic," placing a high value on schedules, punctuality, and time is segmented into small, precise units. Others are "polychronic," where time is seen as more fluid and focused on relational and event timing rather than the clock. These cultural attitudes can deeply affect how individuals within these societies experience and manage their time.

The tempo of our environment can also manipulate our experience of time. Life in urban settings often feels faster due to the high volume of activities and stimuli we're exposed to. In contrast, time might seem to pass more slowly in rural areas, with fewer distractions and a closer connection to the natural rhythms of days and seasons.

Understanding the subjective nature of time is crucial in the context of time management. By knowing what speeds up or slows down our time perception, we can better manage our engagement with tasks and activities. For instance, breaking down overwhelming projects into smaller, manageable tasks can make time feel more expansive, giving a sense of control and progress.

Ultimately, our perception of time is malleable; with this knowledge, we can employ strategies to make the most out of it. By recognizing that our experience of time is influenced by more than the ticking of a clock, we can shape our perception to enrich our lives. Whether by introducing variety to slow down time's passage, practicing mindfulness to savor the moment, or structuring our days to sync with our natural rhythms, we can experience time in a way that aligns with our goals and well-being.

Part 4 Rethinking Productivity: Output vs. Outcome

In a world where "productivity" often translates to how much one can achieve in the least amount of time, there's a growing need to rethink this concept. The traditional focus on output—measuring productivity by the sheer volume of work done—has dominated the corporate and personal productivity landscapes for years. However, this approach often overlooks the importance of outcome—the actual results and impact of the work completed.

Rethinking productivity requires shifting from a quantity-focused to a quality-focused mindset, where the value of the work produced is prioritized over the volume. This paradigm shift is essential for several reasons.

First, the obsession with output can lead to burnout. When individuals and organizations prioritize the number of tasks completed over the significance of those tasks, they encourage working longer hours, skipping breaks, and, ultimately, unsustainable work habits. While this might boost short-term productivity, in the long term, it can lead to mental and physical exhaustion, decreased quality of work, and lower overall productivity.

Second, an output-focused approach does not account for the

complexity of most tasks. Not all tasks are created equal; some require deep thought, creativity, and problem-solving, while others are more routine. By focusing on the outcome, individuals and organizations can give employees the time and space needed to tackle complex problems effectively, leading to innovative solutions and improvements in quality.

Moreover, an outcome-oriented mindset aligns better with personal and organizational goals. It encourages setting clear objectives and measuring progress against those objectives rather than just ticking off tasks on a to-do list. This approach ensures that every effort is made towards achieving a specific, desired result that is far more meaningful and satisfying for all involved.

Additionally, rethinking productivity to focus on outcomes can foster a more flexible and accommodating work environment. It can lead to the recognition that productivity doesn't necessarily mean being busy or present at a desk for a set number of hours. Instead, it can mean delivering excellent results while maintaining a healthy work-life balance.

This outcome-centric productivity also leverages the strengths of diverse teams. When the quality of work is the metric, there is room to acknowledge and utilize individual talents and ways of working that might not fit into traditional productivity molds. It allows for different but complementary work styles as long as the end goal is achieved with excellent results.

Emphasizing outcomes also means reassessing and often streamlining processes. By focusing on the result, redundant steps in a process can be identified and removed, leaving a more efficient path to the goal. This "lean" approach to productivity saves time, reduces frustration, and conserves energy for the tasks that truly matter.

To effectively implement this shift, goals must be specific, measurable, achievable, relevant, and time-bound (SMART). This framework ensures that outcomes are well-defined and that progress can be objectively measured. Regular reviews and feedback loops can help ensure that efforts are on track and adjustments can be made as necessary.

Technology plays a significant role in rethinking productivity.

Automation and artificial intelligence can handle repetitive tasks, freeing humans to focus on more complex and strategic work that results in meaningful outcomes. This improves efficiency and enhances job satisfaction by allowing employees to engage in more rewarding work.

The shift from output to outcome requires a fundamental change in mindset and culture. It's about redefining what it means to be productive, moving away from the antiquated industrial model of productivity as a measure of time spent working to a more modern, human-centric approach that values the impact and quality of work.

This change can lead to more sustainable work practices, greater innovation, and a more engaged workforce. It's about working smarter, not harder, and recognizing that the true measure of productivity is not how much we can do but how well we do it and how it impacts the real world.

CHAPTER 3

ASSESSING YOUR TIME-ANXIETY PROFILE

Assessing your time-anxiety profile is essential to understanding how time-related stress affects you and determining the best strategies to manage it. This self-assessment requires a reflective and honest look at how you interact with time daily.

Start by examining your thoughts and feelings about time. Do you constantly worry about being late or missing deadlines, even when you're on schedule? Does the end of the day often leave you feeling like you haven't done enough? Pay attention to physical sensations, too—does thinking about your to-do list quicken your heartbeat or create a knot in your stomach?

Reflect on your behaviors surrounding time. Are you a chronic procrastinator, or do you tend to over-schedule yourself to the point of overload? How do you react when an unforeseen event disrupts your carefully planned schedule? Identifying these patterns is crucial; they indicate your relationship with time.

Consider how your perception of time affects your productivity and well-being. Are you often caught in a cycle of rush and restlessness, feeling like there's never enough time, which paradoxically leads to inefficient work and wasted time? Or do you underestimate the time tasks will take, leading to a constant state of catch-up?

It's also important to acknowledge the impact of external pressures on your time anxiety. The influence of workplace culture, societal expectations, and even familial responsibilities can all contribute to how you experience and manage time.

By assessing your time-anxiety profile, you gain insights into the roots of your time-related stress. This knowledge empowers you to implement tailored time management techniques, set realistic expectations, and develop a more compassionate approach to allocating your time—ultimately leading to a calmer, more centered, and productive life.

Part 1 Identifying Your Time-Anxiety Triggers

Time anxiety can manifest differently from person to person, but it is often rooted in specific triggers—events or thoughts that precipitate a disproportionate concern about time and its passage. To alleviate time anxiety, it's essential first to identify these triggers.

Common time anxiety triggers include looming deadlines, a packed schedule, or an unexpected task that throws off your carefully planned routine. It's not just the large-scale events, either; even daily time checks or the ding of a new email can prompt anxiety in some individuals. The key lies in pinpointing exactly which situations are causing you stress and then examining why.

For some, the trigger might be a fear of being late, which stems from a deeper worry about social judgment or letting others down. For others, it may be a consequence of perfectionism, where the desire to complete every task flawlessly creates unrealistic expectations about how much time spent on a single task is justifiable.

To identify your triggers, start by observing the patterns in your daily life. When do you feel your heart rate increase, or your mood sink at the thought of time? Is it during the morning rush when the day's obligations loom large? Or perhaps in the evening when you reflect on what you've accomplished that day? Record these observations in a journal, noting the time of day and the context of your anxiety. Over time, a pattern will likely emerge. (Instructions at the end of this chapter.)

Once you have identified potential triggers, delve deeper into their origins. Ask yourself probing questions: What about this situation is causing stress? Are there underlying fears or beliefs at play? It could be a fear of failure, a dread of missing out, or even a deep-seated belief that one's worth is tied to productivity.

For instance, if you find that checking your watch frequently is a trigger, it could be that you're worried about not making the most of your time. It could also mean that you have a warped perception of how much one person can achieve. This concern may originate from an internalized pressure always to be productive, a common theme in today's society.

Additionally, consider whether your time anxiety is linked to past experiences. Perhaps previous consequences of poor time management, like missing a deadline or arriving late to an important event, are haunting you. These past events can reinforce the fear that history will repeat itself, thus escalating your anxiety whenever a similar situation arises.

With triggers identified and understood, the next step is to confront them directly. This might involve challenging irrational thoughts and beliefs about time with evidence from your own experiences. For example, if the fear of being late is a significant trigger, remind yourself of the times you have arrived early or on time and were able to handle the situation successfully.

Developing healthier coping strategies is crucial. If a jam-packed schedule is a trigger, learn to prioritize tasks and, importantly, learn the self-preservationist art of saying "no" to non-essential commitments. If unexpected tasks trigger anxiety, practice flexible thinking to accommodate changes without panic. Flexible thinking is the ability to think about a situation in a different way. It involves reframing so you can accept things outside your control. For example, at first evaluation, a last-minute delay to a presentation appointment for new business might seem inconvenient. On the flipside, it can also be seen as an opportunity to fine tune the pitch with colleagues, and also puts you in the position of having accommodated the potential client already. This rewiring takes time, but mindfulness and relaxation techniques can also help manage the physiological responses to time anxiety.

It's essential to be patient with yourself. Identifying and addressing your time-anxiety triggers is not an overnight process, but rather an ongoing journey of self-discovery and adjustment. As you learn more about your patterns and implement strategies, you'll gradually see improvements in your relationship with time. (You will find step-by-step instructions for a reflective process to identify your triggers at the end of this chapter.)

Common triggers for time anxiety include:

Deadlines

The most obvious trigger for time anxiety is an upcoming deadline. Whether for work, school, or personal projects, the pressure to complete tasks by a specific date can cause significant stress. The closer the deadline, the more intense the anxiety can become, especially if you feel unprepared or behind schedule.

Overcommitment

Saying yes to too many obligations can lead to a packed schedule with little breathing room. This over-commitment often results from an inability to estimate how long tasks will take, a desire to please others, or difficulty saying no. The consequent lack of free time can lead to a constant state of rush and overwhelm.

Perfectionism

Perfectionists often struggle with time anxiety because they set unrealistically high standards for themselves and the work they produce. They may spend excessive time on tasks, trying to make everything perfect, leading to delays and a heightened sense of urgency as deadlines approach.

Procrastination

Ironically, avoidance of tasks due to underlying fears or a lack of motivation can lead to time anxiety. Procrastination can cause a snowball effect; the more you delay, the more anxious you become about the limited time left to complete your tasks.

Multitasking

Attempting to handle multiple tasks simultaneously can trigger time anxiety, often leading to lower productivity and a sense that you're never fully completing anything. This constant juggling can make it feel like there's never enough time to do everything well.

Comparisons with Others

Observing peers who seem to accomplish more or manage their time better can trigger feelings of inadequacy and anxiety. This comparison can create a sense that you are not using your time as effectively as others.

Life Transitions

Significant life changes such as starting a new job, going to school, or a significant event in your personal life like marriage or the birth of a child can disrupt your routine and lead to anxiety about managing your time with these new responsibilities.

Technology and Connectivity

The constant barrage of notifications and the pressure to be always available can exacerbate time anxiety. The digital age has blurred the lines between work and personal time, often leading to a sense that you must be productive every minute of the day.

Lack of Prioritization

Without clear priorities, it can be challenging to decide what to work on first, which can trigger anxiety. The feeling that everything is important and urgent can lead to paralysis and feeling overwhelmed.

Negative Self-Talk

Internal dialogue that reinforces the idea that you're not doing enough or that you're always behind can perpetuate time anxiety. This negative self-talk can create a cycle of stress and decreased productivity.

Part 2 Identifying Your Time-Anxiety Profile

We're all racing against the clock these days and feeling anxious about time is pretty common. It's like there's this constant pressure, a feeling that we're always running late, always trying to catch up with time. But this worry about time looks different for everyone. Getting to know the different types of time stress is key to finding ways to deal with it that really work for us.

Image: Get to know your reactive time stress patterns and stay in front!

Let's take a closer look at these types of time stress. Some of us try to do too much and end up stretched too thin. Others aim for everything to be perfect and can never quite get there. Then there are those who put things off until the last minute, those who get lost in their phones and computers, and those who plan everything but still feel out of control.

Understanding these patterns is not just about putting labels on them; it's about seeing a bit of ourselves in these stories and figuring out how to make peace with time. It's about changing how we see time—from something we never have enough of, to something we have plenty of. So, let's start this journey to understand better, not just to get better at managing time, but to enjoy our lives more.

The experience of time anxiety can vary greatly from person to person, influenced by individual lifestyles, values, and pressures. Here are several profile types that represent different groups of time-anxious individuals:

The Over-Committer:

Characteristics: Often says yes to every request, leading to an overcrowded schedule.

Time-Anxiety Trigger: Fear of missing out or letting others down.

The Perfectionist:

Characteristics: Spends excessive time on tasks, aiming for flawless execution.

Time-Anxiety Trigger: Fear of making mistakes and being judged by others.

The Procrastinator:

Characteristics: Regularly puts off tasks, leading to a rush to meet deadlines.

Time-Anxiety Trigger: Avoidance of difficult tasks or decision-making fatigue.

The Crisis Manager:

Characteristics: Thrives on last-minute pressures but feels constant anxiety.

Time-Anxiety Trigger: Hooked into the adrenaline rush of urgent deadlines, which leads to poor planning.

The Busy Bee:

Characteristics: Finds identity in being busy, often equating busyness with self-worth.

Time-Anxiety Trigger: Social validation and a sense of accomplishment from being perpetually active.

The Multi-Tasker:

Characteristics: Juggles multiple tasks at once, leading to fragmented attention.

Time-Anxiety Trigger: A belief that doing more equals greater productivity.

The Dreamer:

Characteristics: Has many ideas and goals but struggles to prioritize and take action.

Time-Anxiety Trigger: Overwhelm from too many big dreams and projects and lack of concrete planning.

The Tech Addict:

Characteristics: Constantly connected to digital devices, leading to a reactive lifestyle.

Time-Anxiety Trigger: Fear of missing out on information and digital updates.

The Role Juggler:

Characteristics: Balances multiple roles such as parent, worker, partner, leading to a life spent trying to stretch the hours in the day to accommodate the overload. (Just in case I need to say it: you can't actually stretch time, only your tolerance.)

Time-Anxiety Trigger: The challenge of fulfilling expectations in all life domains.

The People Pleaser:

Characteristics: Prioritizes others' needs and expectations over personal time management.

Time-Anxiety Trigger: Desire for approval and fear of confrontation or conflict.

The Planner:

Characteristics: Spends excessive time planning and organizing, seeking control over time.

Time-Anxiety Trigger: Uncertainty and the unpredictability of life events.

The Leisure Seeker:

Characteristics: Desires ample free time and leisure but feels guilty or anxious when taking it.

Time-Anxiety Trigger: Internalized societal pressure to be always productive.

Strategies Targeted to Specific Time-Anxiety Profiles

Now that you have identified your Time-Anxiety Profile, you can tailor your response using the following guidelines. Each of these profiles requires a tailored approach to managing time anxiety, involving strategies that address the specific behaviors and thought patterns contributing to your stress around time. Whether it's learning to delegate, setting more realistic expectations, or incorporating mindfulness practices, there are various ways for each type to move towards a more time-affluent lifestyle.

By adopting targeted strategies, each profile type can begin to reshape their approach to time, mitigate anxiety, and move towards a more balanced and fulfilling use of their hours.

The Over-Committer:

Learn to prioritize tasks based on importance and not just urgency, using tools like the Eisenhower Matrix.

Practice saying "no" or "let me get back to you" to avoid instant commitments, allowing time to assess your schedule.

The Perfectionist:

Set clear and realistic standards for tasks, and practice accepting "good enough" when appropriate.

Use time-blocking to allocate a fixed amount of time for tasks, preventing endless tweaking and revisions.

The Procrastinator:

Break tasks into smaller, manageable steps to reduce overwhelm and make the starting stage less intimidating.

Implement the two-minute rule— if something takes less than two minutes, do it immediately.

The Crisis Manager:

Develop a routine for regular planning and preparation to avoid reliance on last-minute stress.

Schedule tasks well ahead of deadlines to distribute work more evenly over time.

The Busy Bee:

Reflect on personal values to align your activities with what truly matters, rather than filling time with busywork.

Schedule your downtime deliberately; treat it with the same importance as other appointments.

The Multi-Tasker:

Practice single-tasking to improve your focus and efficiency on one activity at a time.

Use techniques like the Pomodoro Technique to dedicate short, intense focus periods to tasks without switching.

The Dreamer:

Set SMART goals to turn your broad dreams into specific, actionable objectives.

Create a visual roadmap or a timeline for goals to track your progress and maintain your focus.

The Tech-Addict:

Allocate specific times for checking digital devices and use app blockers to minimize distractions.

Engage in tech-free activities that promote concentration and mindfulness, like reading or outdoor exercises.

The Role Juggler:

Delegate and share responsibilities where possible to alleviate the pressure of fulfilling all roles alone.

Establish and communicate clear boundaries for work and family time to ensure dedicated focus for each role.

The People Pleaser:

Practice self-affirmation exercises to bolster confidence in personal decision-making.

Engage in assertiveness training to comfortably express your personal needs and manage others' expectations.

The Planner:

Allow for flexibility in your plans by creating buffer zones to accommodate changes or delays.

Engage in spontaneous activities occasionally to become more comfortable with unpredictability.

The Leisure Seeker:

Recognize the value of rest and leisure for overall productivity and well-being to alleviate associated guilt.

Schedule leisure activities as part of the weekly plan, reinforcing their legitimacy and importance.

Part 3 Self-Assessment: Evaluating Your Time Management Habits

Self-assessment is invaluable for improving time management skills. Evaluating your time management habits involves critically examining how you organize your day, prioritize tasks, and deal with distractions and procrastination. Here's a step-by-step guide to self-assessing your time management habits.

1. Reflect on Your Current Practices

Start by reflecting on your current time management practices. How do you typically plan your day? Do you make to-do lists or set goals? Consider if you have a structured approach to organizing tasks and use any tools or techniques, such as time-blocking or the Pomodoro Technique, to manage your time more effectively.

2. Track Your Time

Before you can manage your time better, you must understand how you spend it. Keep a detailed log of your daily activities for a week or so. This log should include both work and leisure activities. This data lets you identify patterns and see where your time is going.

3. Analyze Your Task Prioritization

Look at how you prioritize your tasks. Are you focusing on urgent tasks at the expense of important ones? Do you know how to tell the difference? Assess your ability to set priorities based on deadlines, the significance of the task, and the potential outcomes of completing (or not completing) a task.

4. Evaluate Distractions and Interruptions

Distractions can be the biggest thieves of time. Assess how often you're distracted and what typically causes it. Is it technology, other people, or your thoughts? How do you handle interruptions? Can you quickly refocus, or are you derailed for lengthy periods?

5. Consider Your Goals and Objectives

Your time management should be aligned with your long-term goals and objectives. Evaluate whether your daily actions move you closer to or further from your goals. Are you spending time on activities that are not contributing to your personal or professional growth?

6. Recognize Procrastination Habits

Be honest with yourself about procrastination. Are there specific tasks that you tend to put off? If so, why? Understand the reasons behind your procrastination. Is it due to a lack of interest, skill, or fear of failure?

7. Assess Your Decision-Making Speed

Consider how long it takes to make decisions. Indecision can be a significant time-waster. Can you make swift, effective decisions, or do you spend too much time deliberating over choices?

8. Inspect Your Work-Life Balance

Assess how well you balance your work and personal life. Are you working late into the night and sacrificing personal time? A lack of balance can lead to burnout, which ultimately harms productivity.

9. Reflect on Your Stress Levels

High stress levels can negatively impact time management. Evaluate if your approach to managing time is causing stress or if high stress levels prevent you from managing time effectively.

10. Create an Action Plan

Based on your assessment, identify areas for improvement. Create an action plan with specific steps to enhance your time management skills. Whether it's adopting new tools and techniques or simply changing your environment, define clear strategies to implement.

Remember that time management is not about squeezing as many tasks into your day as possible; it's about simplifying how you work, getting things done more quickly, and leaving more time for leisure, relaxation, and personal growth. As you conduct your self-assessment, maintain a compassionate and non-judgmental attitude toward yourself. Acknowledge that perfection is not the goal—improvement is. And with consistent effort, your time management habits will improve.

Part 4 The Role of Procrastination and Perfectionism

Procrastination and perfectionism are often seen as direct opposites in terms of productivity and time management, but actually, they frequently coexist. They can also significantly impede an individual's efficiency and well-being. Understanding the interplay between these two habits can be transformative for individuals struggling with time anxiety and time management.

Procrastination: The Thief of Time

Procrastination is a common issue that affects many people across various aspects of their lives. It's delaying or postponing tasks, often against our better judgment. This can stem from various causes, including fear of failure, feeling overwhelmed, a lack of motivation— either from intrinsic or extrinsic sources, but more on that soon—or simply the desire to do something more enjoyable.

Procrastination can also be a response to an ill-defined task or project, where the starting point isn't clear, or the task is too large and unwieldy to contemplate. The cost of procrastination is not just lost time; it can lead to increased stress, reduced performance quality, and decreased personal happiness.

When tasks are postponed, less time is available to complete them, leading to rushed work and errors. This can become a vicious cycle: the anxiety produced by procrastination leads to further procrastination as the individual seeks to avoid the uncomfortable feelings associated with the task.

Perfectionism: The Paralysis of Progress

Perfectionism, on the other hand, is a relentless striving for flawlessness and setting high-performance standards accompanied by overly critical self-evaluations and concerns regarding others' evaluations. While it can lead to impressive achievements, it can also result in a fear of starting or completing tasks, as the individual fears that the result won't meet their high standards.

Perfectionism can lead to significant time management issues. Perfectionists may struggle to complete tasks because they're never quite satisfied with the outcome. They may also avoid starting tasks they fear they won't be able to complete perfectly. This can result in procrastination, where tasks are delayed in the quest for the perfect moment, the perfect condition, or the perfect set of knowledge to complete them.

The Procrastination-Perfectionism Link

Procrastination and perfectionism are often intertwined. A perfectionist may procrastinate to avoid the risk of failure or criticism. At the same time, procrastination can exacerbate perfectionist tendencies, as delaying tasks can lead to a rush to complete them. In a hurry, mistakes are made, reinforcing the fear of imperfection.

In this cycle, time management suffers as the individual becomes trapped in a pattern of avoidance and rushed completion. This not only impacts the individual's productivity but also their mental health, as the stress and anxiety associated with both procrastination and perfectionism take their toll.

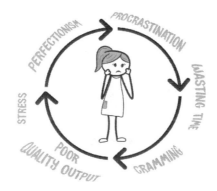

Image: Break free from the procrastination-perfectionism cycle!

In time management, these behaviors are critical. Perfectionism can lead to procrastination, as perfectionists put off completing tasks, due to unrealistic expectations, or a sense that more time is needed to achieve the quality of work desired. These delaying tactics lead to a misuse of time: time wasting and cramming tasks at the last minute, which can affect the quality of work and induce significant stress.

We've already discussed what is happening in the primal parts of our brains when we are stressed, so it's no surprise that we are not doing our best work when cramming. In practical terms, poor time management can disrupt schedules, interfere with long-term planning, and ultimately result in missed opportunities and deadlines.

While perfectionism can lead to high-quality outcomes, it often results in inefficiency. Excessive time devoted to perfecting a single task could be distributed across numerous tasks. This imbalance can lead to work not being completed within realistic timeframes, creating a backlog and a sense of never catching up.

Breaking the Cycle

Individuals must learn to recognize their patterns and triggers to manage the detrimental effects of procrastination and perfectionism on time management. Cognitive-behavioral therapy (CBT) strategies provide an excellent framework to challenge and reframe the irrational thoughts that often underlie these behaviors. An example of CBT at work would be to bring awareness to progress-limiting self-talk, such as "If I can't do this perfectly, I won't do it at all," and purposefully and consciously replacing it with "Done is better than perfect."

It's also essential to break tasks into smaller, more manageable steps to reduce the overwhelm that can lead to procrastination. By creating mini goals that are achievable, we are not only setting realistic performance standards, we are achieving them, leading to a sense of satisfaction that motivates us to tackle the next section of the project. I once discussed motivation and task completion approaches with a successful CEO, who told me he places "drink water" on his "to-do list" several times a day—among other seemingly insignificant and mundane goals. He said that just the visual of checked off items supported his sense of achievement.

I interpreted this as a powerful self-psychology measure; he was mitigating the paralyzing effects of perfectionism that might have plagued him if he'd only seen how many of the more complex tasks were yet to be completed. Pragmatic solutions support the psychological, and time management techniques such as the Pomodoro Technique or time-blocking can help individuals get started on tasks and maintain a healthy pace of work without succumbing to the all-or-nothing mentality.

This concept of mentality is key. Much of your procrastination-perfectionism cycle could have its roots in underlying beliefs established during childhood so it's important to analyze your responses to success and failure—both past and present. There are two broad types of motivation, differentiated by their source. One comes from within, from our own aspirations, enjoyment of tasks, and alignment between our work and our own self-concept—motivation experts call this "intrinsic motivation."

Extrinsic motivation is external. For an adult, this might include salary increase opportunities, a new office, and/or public praise or acknowledgement. These are forms of positive reinforcement, but the opposite can also be motivating, such as the fear of not progressing in your career or losing your job entirely, or just a public dressing down in the boardroom. For a child, this was stickers and treats, or conversely, detention and being grounded. This teaches children to look outside of themselves for a reason to do something or not do something, and parents and teachers teach this lesson well, and it sticks.

This ingrained habit of looking outwards for a pat on the back or working to avoid "punishment" distracts us from our natural, intrinsic motivation to develop and create—something that must be innate or humans would never have done so much (often inessential) creating. Once we know we have this tendency to search for outside validation or censure to guide the pace or quality of our task completion, we can use CBT strategies to tease out the self-talk that is steering us away from our internal drive to reach our goals. It also replaces the fear-fueled mantras with empowering ones.

Many of the triggers discussed in Part 3 originate from our externalized motivation, one way or the other. Think "People-pleaser" and "Perfectionist" for the ones who want the pat on the back and think

"Procrastinator" and "Multi-tasker" for those who (mostly subconsciously) respond with a sense of resistance to external compulsion, as it brings up a sense of perceived coercion. Sometimes this ingrained habit of responding to societal pressures can be difficult to unravel. Still, signs can include a hyperfocus on how other people see your achievements and externalized motivation (only doing things if you have to). Many people have a mixture of causes, so it's important to tease out your reasons.

Just try writing down your thoughts next time you are struggling with a deadline and see who or what features in your notebook. Is it you and your deep desire to meet the deadline, or is it what people will think or say (or do) as a result of your "failure"? Does it bring up anything from the past? School experiences?

The Impact on Well-being

Both procrastination and perfectionism can harm mental health. The stress and anxiety associated with the constant delay and the self-imposed pressure of perfectionism can lead to burnout, depression, and a perpetual sense of dissatisfaction. There's also the emotional toll of constantly living under the stress of impending deadlines and self-criticism.

Managing Procrastination and Perfectionism

Addressing these behaviors begins with awareness and self-compassion. The first step is recognizing the triggers and irrational beliefs that fuel procrastination and perfectionism. Time management strategies can then be applied more effectively. Setting realistic goals, breaking tasks into manageable steps, and focusing on progress rather than perfection are tactics that can help.

Cognitive-behavioral techniques can be particularly beneficial in dealing with the underlying thought patterns. Learning to challenge perfectionist thinking and accepting that mistakes are a part of the learning process is essential. For procrastination, techniques like the "five-minute start" can help by encouraging engagement with a task for just five minutes, often leading to longer periods of productivity.

To deal with procrastination and trying to be perfect, we need a careful plan to understand the deep feelings and thoughts involved. By using specific methods, people can manage their time better, feel less worried, get more done, and be happier with their work and personal life.

Part 5 Understanding Your Chronotype and Productivity Peak

Understanding your chronotype is key to optimizing your productivity. A chronotype refers to an individual's natural inclination toward the timing of their sleep and wake cycles. Identifying your chronotype can reveal your productivity peaks—when you're most alert and capable of producing your best work. This understanding is crucial for effective time management and can be particularly beneficial for those who struggle with time anxiety.

The Science of Chronotypes

Chronotypes are part of our genetic makeup and are influenced by the circadian rhythms that regulate the sleep-wake cycle. Taxonomies vary but there are generally three types: morning (larks), evening (owls), and neither (third birds). Larks wake up energized and are most productive in the first half of the day. Owls, in contrast, peak in the evening. Thirdly, birds have more flexibility but still tend to have a specific window where they are more productive.

Research conducted with elite athletes found that chronotype profile significantly affected the performance of athletes in the areas of "daytime sleepiness, psychomotor vigilance, executive function and isometric grip strength." Performance was "significantly impaired" on all measures when athletes trained outside their body's preferred "phase." "Night owl" athletes, for example, responded much less positively to early morning timed training sessions and struggled to reach the peak performance they enjoyed during afternoon physical assessments.

Obviously, this has implications for elite athlete and sporting coaching teams, for whom early mornings are an established norm. Of course, it is interesting to wonder if many of these night owls might have been organically "weeded out," considering the propensity for elite sports training to occur prior to school and working commitments. Regardless, this research can equally be applied to any activity that requires productivity for one key reason: it measured executive function, the complex cognitive skill that basically runs our lives.

Executive functioning covers three main cognitive functions. The first is "inhibition," which relates to "suppressing inappropriate or incorrect responses," such as choosing not to do something, or pushing down the wrong words (or harsh words) in favor of a more positive and productive communication. The second is "updating and operating memory"; poor performance in this area impacts our ability to quickly remember concepts and processes, and manage our list of competing priorities. Importantly, this also slows the storage of new learning experiences as concrete knowledge, reducing productivity and slowing our progress at work.

Finally—and crucially in a modern world—our brain needs to do something called "shifting," which means moving from one response or process to another. This aspect of executive function is responsible for tasks that require mental agility ranging from communication to problem-solving.

Our ability to "switch" governs everything from communication to analysis and problem-solving. In each case, we are required to hold several elements in our working memory and switch between them. As previously discussed, the multitasking myth that we are actually doing two things at once, is actually just superfast switching between tasks. Our ability to do this will be either impaired or sharpened, depending on the time of day, which is why chrono-typing is so powerful.

Switching deficiency could affect our capacity for the unavoidable "multitasking" or task-switching required for contemporary business environments. This might include the ability to switch between modes; referring to a written report and then discussing it verbally in a meeting requires critical thinking and mode switching, all executive functions. Impaired switching could also mean that the code-switching needed for intercultural business communications is less fluid, or that we struggle to understand others' perspectives during negotiations or planning meetings. Essentially, the morning lark's 7 p.m. dip in mental agility may impact their capacity to negotiate a tense business meeting or solve a roadblock in a project, while a night owl will experience the same deficiencies at a breakfast meeting.

With this sort of impact on productivity, it's worth working out where you fit in this matrix of chronotypes. Recognizing your chronotype allows you to align your tasks with your natural energy levels. For example, if you're a lark, tackling the most demanding tasks in the morning and leaving routine or less intensive tasks for the afternoon could improve your efficiency and quality of work.

Assessing Your Chronotype

To determine your chronotype, reflect on what times you naturally wake up and feel tired, without the influence of alarm clocks or evening social activities. There are also quizzes and assessments developed by sleep researchers that can provide insight into your natural tendencies.

Productivity Peaks and Valleys

Once you understand your chronotype, you can start to plan your day around your peaks and valleys. During your peak times, you should engage in work that requires focus and critical thinking. Conversely, when you're in a valley or less energetic phase, it's the perfect time to schedule meetings, administrative tasks, or other low-intensity activities.

For instance, your peak might be between 8 a.m. and noon if you're a morning person. This is when you should focus on tasks that are high priority or require more concentration. An evening person might find their peak between 2 p.m. and 6 p.m., or even later, and should thus schedule their most important tasks accordingly. I actually think these chronotypes should be discussed with high school and university students, or really anyone who is just starting out on career development. Think of how much angst a night owl might save by realizing they might never adjust to the early mornings in the military or elite sports coaching.

Adapting to the Workday

Having said that, if the intrinsic motivation for a particular career is strong, then a person can use external supports, such as planning tools or even blackout curtains and brown noise to adjust their chronotype to the time of day they need to be productive.   Similarly, many industries follow the traditional workday rhythms, so comprehensive change to your working hours may not even be possible. So, while it's ideal to align your work with your chronotype, if you're faced with a fixed work schedule or other commitments, it's important to find smaller ways to adapt. This might involve using light therapy to shift your circadian rhythms or taking strategic breaks to recharge during dips in your energy levels. It could just be managing your intra-daily routine to maximize productivity.

Managing Time Anxiety with Chronotype Awareness

Time anxiety can be exacerbated when you feel like you're not working at your best. You can reduce the stress associated with underperformance or time pressure by syncing your tasks with your productivity peaks. This also allows for a more realistic estimation of how long tasks will take, as you'll work when you are naturally more efficient.

The practical application of implementing chronotype-aware scheduling involves:

- Planning intensive tasks during peak productivity periods

- Arranging low-intensity tasks for off-peak times

- Taking short, restorative breaks during energy troughs to maintain a productivity baseline

- Adjusting your environment to support energy levels, such as exposure to natural light for morning types or quiet, dimly lit spaces for evening types in the morning

You can improve efficiency and reduce time anxiety by leveraging your chronotype and planning your day accordingly. This harmonization between biological predispositions and daily activities enables a smoother, more productive flow through the day, leading to a calmer, more controlled approach to time management.

CHAPTER 4
PRINCIPLES OF TIME-AFFLUENCE

Time affluence is having sufficient time to pursue personally meaningful activities, reflect, engage in leisure, innovate, and simply be present in the moment. It's less about managing every second and more about prioritizing quality and fulfillment over mere busyness.

The principles of time affluence center around prioritizing tasks and understanding that time, like money, is a resource that can be managed and allocated according to one's values and goals.

The first step is to prioritize time over material possessions, recognizing that experiences and time for leisure, self-improvement, and relationships contribute more significantly to well-being than tangible goods. Too often time is seen as a legitimate sacrifice for the accrual of wealth.

Another principle is intentionality, the conscious allocation of time to align with one's values and goals rather than succumbing to the urgency of the "busy" trap. Mindfulness also plays a key role, encouraging a present-oriented focus that appreciates each moment rather than always looking ahead to the next task. Additionally, there's an emphasis on autonomy, having control over your time and choosing how it is spent, rather than being at the mercy of external demands. This ties in with the quest to connect with your own intrinsic motivation (discussed in Chapter 3, Part 4).

Lastly, there's a practice of saying no, setting boundaries to protect time, and investing it where it truly counts. Together, these principles cultivate a sense of abundance in time, leading to a richer and more fulfilling life.

Part 1 Embracing the Slow Movement: Quality Over Speed

In a world that values quick results and immediate satisfaction, the Slow Movement emerges as a countercultural revolution that stresses pacing ourselves to enrich our quality of life. This movement is not about doing everything at a snail's pace but seeking to do everything at the right speed. It means taking the time to engage in activities that bring us joy, to focus on quality rather than quantity, and to appreciate the moments that make up our lives.

The Philosophy of Slowness

The Slow Movement has its roots in the Slow Food initiative, which began in Italy as a protest against the opening of a fast-food chain near the Spanish Steps in Rome. It advocates taking the time to fully engage with our activities, whether cooking a meal from scratch, engaging in leisurely social activities, or taking the longer scenic route on our commute. It's a rejection of the fast-paced "more is better" mindset that has permeated modern culture, where speed is often prioritized at the expense of quality, health, and well-being.

Reclaiming Time

In embracing slowness, we reclaim our time as our own. This doesn't necessarily mean reducing productivity; rather, it's about ensuring that speed does not compromise quality. By slowing down, we allow ourselves the space to be present in the moment and to perform tasks with intention and attention. This can lead to better outcomes, whether it's a more enjoyable meal, a project completed with greater care, or a more meaningful conversation.

Quality of Experience

The slow movement strongly emphasizes the quality of experience. It's not just about doing less but fully immersing oneself in each experience. By savoring our experiences, we find greater satisfaction and produce better results. In creative work, for instance, this might mean letting ideas mature rather than rushing to meet self-imposed or external deadlines.

Health and Well-being

The health benefits of slow movement are profound. Chronic stress from living life in the fast lane can lead to a host of health problems, from insomnia to heart disease. Slowing down helps to reduce stress and its associated risks. It also encourages practices that improve well-being, like mindfulness and meditation, allowing us to cultivate a state of calm and centeredness.

Environmental Impact

Slowing down also has environmental benefits. The fast-paced consumption of goods is depleting resources and damaging our planet. The slow movement encourages a more sustainable lifestyle, one that values long-lasting quality goods over disposable products and thoughtful consumption over mindless materialism.

Community and Relationships

The slow movement fosters deeper community ties and relationships. It promotes spending quality time with family and friends, engaging in meaningful conversations, and participating in community events. By slowing down, we build stronger, more connected communities.

Implementing Slowness

To embrace slowness, start with small steps. It might mean setting aside technology for a certain part of the day, dedicating time to hobbies without rushing, or simply taking a few deep breaths before beginning a new task. It could also involve bigger life changes, like downsizing to reduce financial stress or working less to enjoy more personal time.

Challenges and Balance

The challenge of adopting slow movement in a fast-paced world is real. It requires a conscious effort to resist societal pressures that equate busyness with importance. Balance is key. Slowness does not mean disregarding time-sensitive responsibilities but finding a pace that allows for excellence, enjoyment, and health.

A Call to Action

Embracing the slow movement is a call to action, a challenge to redefine what it means to live a good life. It's an invitation to find joy in the process rather than rushing towards the outcome, value human connections over efficiency, and respect our limits. In doing so, we don't just enhance our lives; we contribute to a cultural shift that values human well-being over perpetual growth. In essence, the slow movement isn't about doing everything slowly; it's about doing everything mindfully.

Part 2 Principle of Presence: Being "Here Now" Reduces Anxiety

In the relentless pursuit of long-term and short-term goals, the present moment often slips away from us. This detachment from the now can be a significant contributor to time anxiety—the pervasive worry that there's never enough time to do all we want or need to do. The idea of being completely present and in the moment serves as a powerful remedy for today's hectic lifestyle, providing a peaceful refuge in the midst of our continuously busy lives.

The Power of Now

Eckhart Tolle explains in his book, *The Power of Now*, that it's important to understand that the current moment is all we truly possess. "Realize deeply that the present moment is all you have. Make the NOW the primary focus of your life."

The "now" is the only reality we can be sure of, and the only moment that is guaranteed to be influenced by our present actions. While many of our current actions can influence our future, we can't always be sure of that. Nor can we be sure of how they will influence our future, even if they do. This means that by focusing on the present moment we are present for the moments we can guarantee. As Tolle says, "the present moment is all you have".

When we focus on the present moment, we step away from our regrets, nostalgia, and worries and fears for the future. While a focus on possible future obstacles can be the hallmark of good planning, clarity can often get away from us—with our overactive imaginations creating worst-case scenarios that never eventuate. This focus on the "now" has profound implications for our mental well-being. It reduces the noise of constant thought patterns that loop around to obsessing over events we can neither change nor accurately predict. This mental space can then be reallocated to more productive pursuits.

Mindfulness: The Vehicle to Presence

Mindfulness is the vehicle that transports us to the state of being present. It is observing our thoughts, feelings, and sensations without judgment. It is anchoring our attention to the breath, the sensations in our bodies, or the details of our environment, and through it, we cultivate an awareness that grounds us firmly in the present.

Being Present in Daily Life

Integrating presence into daily life can be transformative. Think about the last time you took a walk. Did your mind ruminate on everything from today's client brief to frustrations at home, or to feelings of guilt that you haven't seen an ageing relative lately? Or are you already wise to your brain's habits and you plugged your ears with a podcast to calm the noise? Being present can turn mental chaos into an enriching experience where you suddenly notice those intricate patterns on newly sprouted leaves, the softness of the breeze, or the rhythmic tap of shoes on the pavement. Such a simple shift in focus can significantly reduce feelings of anxiety, as the mind is allowed to take a break from its usual patterns of worry.

Reducing Anxiety

Anxiety often stems from a disconnection from the present moment. When we are present, we are not worrying about a deadline next week or rehashing an argument from yesterday. Instead, we are engaged with the task at hand. This engagement allows for a flow state where time seems to disappear, and we perform at our best. In presence, the grip of anxiety loosens, as the mind is no longer projecting into an uncertain future or clinging to an unchangeable past.

Cultivating a Practice

Being truly present is a social "practice", and any new practice needs to be cultivated. It requires focused intention and, often, a change in habits. It could start with dedicating a few minutes daily to meditation or mindfulness exercises. But more than that, it involves consciously bringing yourself back to the present throughout the day and doing so repeatedly. This is especially important during moments of stress or when we find ourselves slipping into autopilot or damaging self-talk.

When this happens, note the tense of the language in your head. Are you using the past tense? "Beth **went** crazy last time I was late with one of these briefs" (Living in the past: How do we know Beth will do that again, when the circumstances may be different?). When we focus anxiously on the past, we inadvertently reduce our present productivity as our attention is redirected to things we simply cannot change. Let's look at the future thinking now. "If I don't get this done today, I **will run** late on the next project. Then what **will I do**?" Spiraling into fear of things that haven't and might never happen also distracts you from being present with your current task, stealing your focus and, yes, you guessed it, reducing your productivity.

Eckard Tolle would tell us to give ourselves a simple reminder.

"Be here now."

Then, try replacing these distracting thoughts with present-focused positive affirmations like: "I am doing the best I can" or "I know how to do this stuff and I am working well" or "I am good at this stuff. I am creating".

Impact on Time Management

For time management, it is vital that we don't waste time spiraling into powerless or self-destructive thoughts. The principle of presence is incredibly effective for keeping us on task. A mind focused on the present is not procrastinating or rushing through tasks to get to some future point. Tasks are completed more efficiently and with greater care because the full weight of our attention is on what we are doing right now. We are also more relaxed, because we are only processing real circumstances instead of imagined future ones, or past events tinged with trauma.

Presence in Relationships

Notably, presence is equally transformative in our interactions with others. Being fully present with another person, listening intently without planning the next thing to say, creates deeper and more meaningful connections. Often referred to as "active listening", this type of presence enhances communication and positive connection. It also reduces the likelihood of misunderstandings that often lead to anxiety and stress.

Challenges and Rewards

Living with presence is not without its challenges. The mind is a time-traveler by nature, and the lure of the past and future can be strong. However, the rewards of persistence are immense. A present-focused life is richer, fuller, and more peaceful. We feel more in control of our circumstances, because, as we've already discussed, the present is the only time we *know* we can influence. Being present transforms our experience of time from a constant race against the clock to a series of moments to be savored and lived fully.

Embracing Presence

By embracing the principle of presence, we don't just manage our time better; we alter our relationship with time itself. Time anxiety diminishes as we stop measuring our lives by the clock ticking and start experiencing them moment by moment. Presence teaches us that life, in all its fullness, is happening right here and right now—and that's a powerful remedy for anxiety.

Part 3 The Power of Single-Tasking

In the age of digital multitasking, where the ability to juggle numerous tasks simultaneously is often glorified, the power of single-tasking emerges as an almost revolutionary concept. Single-tasking, the practice of dedicating oneself to a single task at a time, aligns seamlessly with the human brain's wiring—enhancing focus, bolstering productivity, and reducing stress.

The Myth of Multitasking

Modern technology has facilitated an environment where multitasking is possible and often encouraged. Contrary to popular belief, the human brain doesn't like multitasking. We're not actually wired for simultaneously handling multiple complex tasks. We think we are doing several things at once, but we're actually rapidly shifting between tasks. This constant switching is taxing on the brain and can lead to increased levels of cortisol, the stress hormone, while hampering productivity. What is so fascinating is that switching between tasks uses the very fuel we need to focus on and complete our tasks (oxygenated glucose)—and it burns it fast, so we feel much more exhausted than we would have if we'd just worked on one task at a time. When we split our attention in this way, and rapidly burn the fuel we need to think, we reduce efficiency and make more mistakes. According to neuroscientist, Daniel J Levitin, the quality of work is compromised up to 40%.

Embracing Single-Tasking

Conversely, single-tasking means fully committing to one activity, giving it undivided attention until completion, or for a set period. It might mean putting your phone on Do Not Disturb for most contacts, removing yourself from open plan environments when completing complex individual tasks and giving yourself a period of time to work on just one thing. This focus maximizes the brain's cognitive resources, leading to better performance and higher-quality outcomes. When we single-task, we enter a state of flow more easily—the optimal psychological state where a person is fully immersed in a task, leading to increased creativity and satisfaction.

Benefits of Single-Tasking

The benefits of single-tasking are multifaceted and relate to brain's processes for managing complex tasks. As we've already discussed, singular focus means deeper focus, and this deeper concentration is critical for complex problem-solving and learning new information. Focusing on one task at a time makes information processing more effective at the time and makes us more likely to store new information in our memory for later retrieval. When we single-task, we adopt a more mindful approach to work and life, where each task is done with intention and awareness, improving the quality of our work, but also how we feel about it. It not only works better, it also feels better.

Reducing Stress and Enhancing Well-being

Single-tasking can significantly mitigate stress. Multitasking often leads to a feeling of constant catch-up, where no single task feels adequately addressed. This can escalate stress levels and lead to burnout. In contrast, focusing and completing a single task provides a sense of control and accomplishment, which can be inherently satisfying and conducive to well-being. This is not only because we are more focused but it's also because we are more likely to finish something. Remember the glasses of water on the CEO's to-do list I mentioned in Chapter 3? Well, single tasking gives us the satisfaction of ticking much more significant things off our lists—instead of having multiple plates still spinning in the air.

Improving Time Management

Single-tasking is also a simple time saver. Just as we waste our brain's energy switching between tasks, we also waste the time it takes to refocus our attention, or even open a different tab. Invariably, we find a rabbit hole for each of the projects, resulting in a day filled with a complex network of rabbit holes and not much done. Put simply, focusing on one task at a time makes you less likely to waste time transitioning between tasks, and reduces the potential rabbit holes you can disappear into. These can add up over the course of a day. This focused approach often results in tasks being completed more quickly and with fewer mistakes, freeing up time that would otherwise be spent on corrections or rework.

Implementing Single-Tasking in Daily Life

Integrating single-tasking into daily life requires intention and practice. It can start with identifying the day's most important task and dedicating time to work on it without interruption. Environmental cues, such as a tidy workspace and the use of headphones to signal to others that you are focusing, can also be helpful. Limiting access to potential distractions, like turning off notifications or having specific times to check emails, supports single-tasking efforts.

Single-Tasking in a Multitasking World

Adopting single-tasking in a world that still values multitasking is challenging. It requires pushing back against cultural norms and work environments that celebrate the myth of "the efficient multitasker". But those who embrace single-tasking often become the true productivity powerhouses, outperforming their multitasking peers.

Long-Term Impact

In the long term, single-tasking can lead to a more fulfilling career and personal life. The depth of work and relationships improves when each aspect of life receives our undivided attention. This depth of connection can foster a sense of competence and achievement, reinforcing the value of single-tasking as a lifelong practice. Importantly, this can provide a positive reinforcement that has originated from within, providing that intrinsic motivation you need to maintain focus and drive.

The power of single-tasking is not just in the work completed but in the peace of mind and clarity it brings. As we reduce the mental clutter of constant task-switching, our capacity for work and enjoyment expands. Single-tasking is a productivity tool and a means to a more focused, satisfying, and purposeful life.

Part 4 The 80/20 Rule Applied to Time Management

The Pareto Principle, commonly known as the 80/20 rule, hypothesizes that roughly 80% of effects come from 20% of causes. When applied to time management, this principle suggests that a small portion of our actions produce most of our results. Harnessing the 80/20 rule can drastically enhance productivity by focusing on what truly matters, significantly improving the efficiency of how time is utilized. Understanding and applying this rule can dramatically improve personal productivity and satisfaction, offering a more strategic approach to allocating our most finite resource: time.

The Origin of the 80/20 Rule

Originally a principle of welfare economics, the term was named after Italian economist Vilfredo Pareto, who in 1906 observed that 80% of Italy's land was owned by 20% of the population. Since then, the 80/20 rule has been applied in various fields, from business to personal productivity. It speaks a universal truth about the imbalance of inputs and outputs; not all effort is equal in its results.

Applied to product marketing, for example, the term has been adopted to describe the phenomenon where a small number of best-selling products dominate, accounting for around 80% of sales in that market. Also explained by Pareto's principle of 80/20 was the idea that about 80% of our business success originates from about 20% of our marketing activity. Identifying which marketing strategies are doing the heavy lifting allows businesses to streamline their marketing activities and discontinue ineffective practices from the marketing budget.

Applying the 80/20 Rule to Time Management

This same thinking can be applied to the way we budget our time. In time management, the 80/20 rule suggests that a small portion of our activities will account for most of our productivity. Identifying which activities make up this critical 20% allows you to prioritize tasks with the greatest impact rather than thinly spreading your effort across all tasks.

Identifying the Vital Few

The first step in applying the rule is to audit how you spend your time. Track your activities and categorize them based on outcomes. You'll likely discover that certain actions, such as strategic planning or deep work sessions, lead to disproportionate gains compared to time spent on emails or meetings.

Eliminating or Delegating the Trivial Many

Once you have identified your vital few tasks, the next step is to examine the remaining 80% of activities that contribute less significantly to your outcomes. These may include tasks that can be automated, delegated, or eliminated. By reducing the time spent on these less impactful activities, you free up more time for those tasks that truly matter.

Strategic Prioritization and Decision-Making

With insight into which tasks are most productive, you can make informed decisions about where to focus your energy. This might mean scheduling your most important tasks during your peak productivity periods or setting strategic goals that align with your 20% activities.

Managing Time and Expectations

Applying the 80/20 rule also involves managing both your time and the expectations of others. It means saying no to tasks that fall outside your vital few and communicating your focus areas to your team or stakeholders.

Overcoming Challenges

One of the main challenges in applying the 80/20 rule is the discomfort of changing habits and pushing back against less productive activities. There might be resistance, both internally and from others when you start to shift your focus. However, consistent application of the principle and communication about its benefits can help overcome these barriers.

80/20 Rule in Personal Life

The principle doesn't just apply to professional tasks. In your personal life, the 80/20 rule can help identify which relationships and activities are most fulfilling so you can invest more time in them.

Continuous Assessment for Efficiency

The 80/20 rule is not a one-time assessment but a continuous process. As your goals and circumstances change, so too will your vital few tasks. Regularly reviewing and adjusting your priorities ensures that you're always aligned with the most effective use of your time.

The 80/20 rule applied to time management is about working smarter, not harder. It's a tool for maximizing productivity, reducing stress, and increasing satisfaction by concentrating on the tasks that significantly impact your goals. By focusing on the powerful 20%, you can transform your workday and your broader life goals, achieving more with less and finding greater balance and fulfillment in the process.

CHAPTER 5
TOOLS AND TECHNIQUES FOR
THE TIME-ANXIOUS

For people who worry about time, learning to manage time well is not just about being efficient; it's the key to unlocking the door to a more peaceful existence. We'll look at many important methods and tools that help calm the mind, and devise strategies to reduce habitual worrying about time.

Integrating these tools and techniques into daily life can transform your relationship with time from anxiety to empowerment. Each of the tasks suggested have the power to lay down new neural pathways about time and productivity. As you practice, you get better at managing your time. These strategies will transform your perception of time from something you worry about to simply a resource to be managed capably and budgeted according to productivity goals. Viewing your time as just another resource to manage transfers the budgeting power back to you, leading to a calmer and more productive life.

Part 1 Time Blocking and the Pomodoro Technique Adapted

Time management is essential in a world where distractions are constant and the pressure to perform is constant. Two techniques, Time Blocking and the Pomodoro Technique, have emerged as beacons of hope for those drowning in the sea of endless tasks. Both methods, when adapted to the individual's working style, can significantly enhance productivity while reducing the anxiety associated with managing time.

Time Blocking: Structuring Your Day for Success

Time Blocking is a calendar-based time management method where you plan out every moment of your day in advance and dedicate specific blocks of time to certain tasks or responsibilities. It transforms the abstract concept of time into a tangible and manageable framework.

Adaptation for Flexibility

For those who find strict schedules daunting, Time Blocking can include flexible blocks where unplanned tasks can be accommodated, thus maintaining a balance between structure and spontaneity. This adaptation can include:

- Buffer Blocks: Interspersing blocks of "free time" between tasks can account for overruns and unexpected demands, reducing the pressure to stick to a rigid schedule.

- Theme Days: Instead of minute-by-minute planning, some may find it more practical to allocate entire days or half-days to broader themes or types of work, such as "Administrative Tuesdays" or "Creative Mornings."

The Pomodoro Technique: The Art of Timed Focus

Another effective management tool is The Pomodoro Technique, developed by Francesco Cirillo. This time management method uses a timer to break work into intervals, traditionally 25 minutes long, separated by short breaks. Each interval is known as a Pomodoro, from the Italian word for "tomato", named after the tomato-shaped kitchen timer Cirillo used as a university student.

Customizing the Pomodoro:

Not everyone can dive deep into a task in 25 minutes, nor will all tasks neatly fit into such intervals. Hence, adapting the Pomodoro Technique is essential for many.

- Variable Intervals: Adjusting the length of the Pomodoros and breaks can cater to different attention spans and task requirements. Some may benefit from 50-minute work intervals with 10-minute breaks, while others may prefer shorter bursts of work.

- Task-Based Pomodoros: Instead of timing the Pomodoro to the minute, some may find it more useful to associate Pomodoros with completing specific tasks or milestones within a project.

Combining Time Blocking with the Pomodoro Technique

By merging Time Blocking with the Pomodoro Technique, individuals can benefit from both structured planning and focused execution. For example, one can block out a two-hour segment for a project and then use the Pomodoro Technique within that block to ensure periods of concentrated work followed by necessary breaks.

Addressing Time Anxiety

The melding of these two methods can significantly alleviate time anxiety. On one level, it's the sense of control that purposeful time management provides, but it also supports attention span regulation as you train your brain to work during certain blocks of time. The psychological benefit of feeling that your life is within your zone of control reduces anxiety, but so do the practical timetabling benefits of the methods.

The Time Blocking aspect ensures a place for everything in your schedule, while the Pomodoro Technique helps maintain focus and prevents burnout. This combination empowers individuals to work with the certainty that their time and energy are being used optimally. It also eliminates decision paralysis about what to work on next, reducing time wasting.

Implementing the Adapted Techniques

To effectively implement these techniques, start by evaluating your current habits and challenges. Identifying periods of high and low energy throughout the day can help in planning Time Blocks more effectively, while recognizing the nature of the tasks at hand can guide the customization of the Pomodoro Technique.

The effectiveness of Time Blocking and the Pomodoro Technique lies in their adaptability. When modified to suit personal productivity rhythms and work styles, they offer a robust framework that can lead to a more disciplined yet flexible approach to time management. The trick is to change how we approach our seemingly endless to-do list. These techniques provide structured, focused work intervals, which require shorter attention spans, and more frequent achievable goals, which means we feel successful more frequently.

Part 2 Mindfulness and Meditation for Time Perception

The relentless pace of modern life often skews our perception of time, making hours seem like minutes and months feel like days. Mindfulness and meditation offer a potent antidote to this distorted time perception, a phenomenon closely linked to time anxiety—the worry that there's never enough time to meet our obligations and fulfill our desires.

Mindfulness: A Foundation for a New Time Perception

Mindfulness is bringing one's attention to experiences occurring in the present moment without judgment. It involves a conscious direction of our awareness away from such things as regrets of the past or worries about the future and on to the now—the only place where time truly exists. The following section explains the key principles of mindfulness and the benefits associated with aligning these principles with your life. These foundations of mindfulness are followed by detailed guidance on how to integrate mindfulness techniques into daily life to achieve these benefits for maximum productive flow and stress reduction.

The Basic Principles of Mindfulness

Meditation: Stretching Time with Intention

Meditation is the practice of using a technique—such as mindfulness or focusing the mind on a particular object, thought, or activity—to train attention and awareness and achieve a mentally clear, emotionally calm, and stable state.

Altered Time Perception: Engaging in mindfulness can lead to a phenomenon known as "time expansion" where one feels that time is passing more slowly, allowing us to savor the moment. This perceived expansion is a direct counter to the feeling of time scarcity that fuels anxiety.

Awareness of Moments: Mindfulness trains us to notice the small things—the texture of a piece of fruit, the sound of a bird, the rhythm of our breath. These moments build up, creating a fuller, richer experience of time.

Reducing Multitasking: By encouraging a single-pointed focus, mindfulness reduces the impulse to multitask, often a response to the fear of time slipping away. This single-tasking makes our experience of time more meaningful and less hurried.

Neurological Impact: Meditation has been shown to affect the brain's perception of time. Regular practitioners often report a subjective feeling of time slowing down as meditation strengthens the brain's prefrontal cortex, the area responsible for executive function, including time assessment.

Reduction of Stress: Meditation lowers stress levels, which can normalize our perception of time. Stress is known to accelerate our internal clock, making meditation a vital practice for decelerating our experience of time.

The Timelessness of Flow: Meditation can induce a state of "flow," an experience where people become so involved in an activity that nothing else seems to matter. Time in a flow state can feel timeless—hours pass like minutes.

Integrating Mindfulness and Meditation into Daily Life

Integrating these practices into daily life can gradually transform our relationship with time. In as little as five minutes a day, we can learn to connect with the present moment, calming the "chatter," which is invariably dominated by inner dialogue about what we've done wrong in the past and what might go wrong in the future.

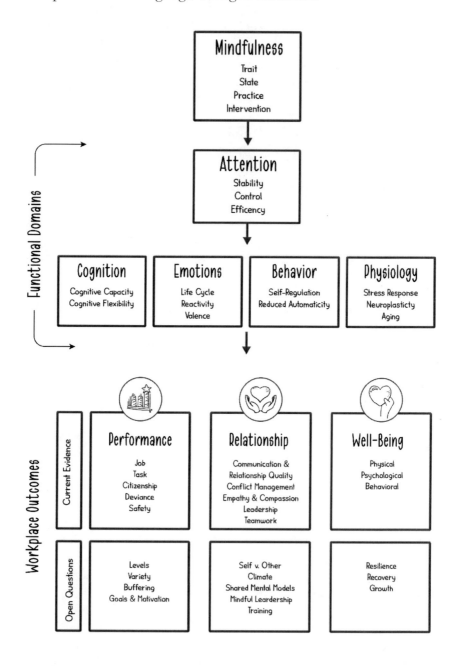

Diagram: Mindfulness regulates the body's processes, improving all aspects of life.

Mindfulness is a difficult area to measure, considering it's an internal process, referring to a metacognitive behavior (thinking about thinking). However, researchers have frequently found a positive correlation between self-reported mindfulness practices and increased productivity. The basis for the impact of mindfulness lies in its impact on our attention, and, in turn, the importance of attention "hygiene" for every aspect of our lives. With its roots in Buddhism, (simply put) mindfulness exercises involve witnessing the noise in your brain but not quite engaging. This way you decenter from negative thoughts, focusing instead on experiential thinking.

So instead of thinking "Is Marco really going to do this again? I might as well just leave, as every time he is in this kind of mood with me, I end up being yelled at for nothing"—you are thinking, "Marco is angry again and I can feel my stomach tightening and a headache forming above my left eye." Bringing awareness to your body, you can then focus on your breath and calm yourself down. These sorts of practices not only improve your focus on the present moment and what you can feel, they discipline your brain (like a Buddhist monk) in practices that enhance stability, control and efficiency—exactly the qualities we want in our work. And how do we bring a touch of Zen into our working lives?

Start Small: Even a few minutes of mindfulness or meditation each day can significantly impact you. A practice as simple as mindful breathing for five minutes can serve as an anchor, bringing a sense of peace and time abundance.

Scheduled Pauses: Regular mindfulness intervals throughout the day can reset our time perception, similar to rebooting a computer that's running too many programs at once.

Mindful Routine Activities: Regular activities like walking or eating can become mindfulness practices. This "informal" mindfulness can help to break the habit of rushing through every task.

Consistent Meditation Practice: Establishing a regular meditation practice, whether seated, walking, or in another form, can deepen the perception of time expansion and strengthen resistance to the psychological pressure of time scarcity.

The Long-Term Effects

Over time, mindfulness and meditation can reshape our time experience. The chronic sense of rush and urgency can give way to a more composed tempo of life. The present moment becomes not a fleeting checkpoint on the way to something else but a space worthy of attention.

Hours and days can be reclaimed by employing mindfulness and meditation to address our skewed perception of time and our emotional reactions to pressure. Sustained practice leads to a more composed, fulfilling experience of life and work. It's a gradual process of re-education for the mind, but we soon learn that by slowing down, we're not losing time but rather enriching the time we have. Through mindfulness and meditation, we learn to explore every corner of each moment and live the full width of time, not just its length.

Part 3 Leveraging Technology: Apps and Tools That Help, Not Hinder

In an era where technology is often seen as a culprit of time anxiety, flipping the narrative to view it as an ally can be transformative. The market is awash with applications and tools designed to streamline our lives and save us from the tyranny of the ever-ticking clock. Here's how to leverage technology to your benefit:

Choosing the Right Tools

The key is not to shun technology but to judiciously select tools that genuinely increase productivity and reduce stress. For every app that might distract, there's another designed to focus the mind and organize the day.

Time-Tracking Apps: Start with time-tracking apps like Toggl or RescueTime. These apps provide insights into where your time is going, helping to identify areas where you can reclaim minutes or even hours for more meaningful activities.

Task Managers: To-do list applications, such as Todoist or Microsoft To Do, help break down tasks into manageable steps. They often feature reminders and categorization that help prioritize and reduce the overwhelm of a crowded schedule.

Calendar Apps: Digital calendars like Google Calendar can sync across all devices, providing reminders for appointments, and can be shared with others for better time coordination.

Focus Aids: Apps like Forest create a virtual tree that grows as you focus, and if you leave the app, the tree withers. Tools that gamify the development of focus and reward your commitment can be a way to stay on track and stay motivated.

Mindfulness and Meditation Apps

Mindfulness and meditation apps, such as Headspace or Calm, offer guided sessions that can help bring a sense of peace and presence into everyday life. They are instrumental in creating a routine around meditation, making it more accessible and less daunting for beginners.

Automation for Efficiency

IFTTT and Zapier: These tools automate repetitive tasks across various apps and services, syncing data, and reducing the need to switch between platforms, thus saving time and reducing digital clutter.

Email Management: Tools like SaneBox and Unroll.Me help manage email overload by filtering important messages and summarizing subscriptions, making the inbox less of a time sink.

Financial Apps: Automate finances with apps like Mint or You Need a Budget (YNAB), which track spending, savings, and budgeting, alleviating the stress and time associated with manual financial management.

Setting Boundaries with Technology

While leveraging technology for better time management, it's equally important to establish boundaries. Harnessing technology effectively requires a conscious and deliberate approach. Here's how to ensure that technology serves as a help rather than a hindrance:

Notification Management: Use Do Not Disturb features or customize notifications to avoid constant interruptions.

Digital Detox: Allocate times for a digital detox, where you disconnect from all devices, helping to reset your attention and avoid digital burnout.

Tech-Free Zones: Create spaces in your home where technology is not allowed, encouraging time spent in reading, conversation, or reflection.

Personalized Technology Use

Lastly, remember that the utility of technology is personal. Customizing the settings, features, and apps to fit your lifestyle and goals is crucial. It's about making the digital world work for you, not control you.

In summary, when used with intention, technology can be a powerful ally in managing time anxiety. By automating mundane tasks, enhancing focus, and facilitating organization, apps and tools can free us to engage more deeply with the moments that matter. It's not about the need to find more time; it's about making the time we have work smarter. Through the strategic use of technology, we can shift from being time-poor to becoming time- and experience-rich.

CHAPTER 6

PRIORITIZATION MASTERY

Mastering the art of prioritization will make you feel as if you've unlocked a secret superpower in today's fast-paced world. This chapter focuses on developing that "sixth sense" about what to do first, so you can contemplate the deluge of tasks coming at you with a sense of calm.

The crucial skill of prioritization mastery is not just about making lists; it's about understanding the difference between what is urgent and what is essential. It's about immediately differentiating "busywork" from activities that lead to true impact. Just as we discussed back in Chapter 4, it's about ensuring you are focusing on the 20% of your work that yields high impact.

With actionable strategies and real-world applications, prioritization mastery isn't about doing more; it's about doing what's necessary—but doing it more efficiently. It's about aligning your daily actions with your long-term goals and values and learning to say a hard "no" to everything else. By the end of this exploration, you will have a set of tools and techniques to prioritize efficiently and the wisdom to apply them with discernment. Prepare to embrace the clarity and focus that come with prioritization mastery and transform the overwhelming into the achievable.

Part 1 The Eisenhower Matrix Revisited

The Eisenhower Matrix, also known as the Urgent-Important Matrix, is a timeless tool that helps users prioritize tasks by urgency and importance, resulting in more efficient time management. Revisiting this classic approach in the context of modern-day productivity can provide renewed insights into managing an increasingly complex workload.

Understanding the Eisenhower Matrix

The Eisenhower Matrix is a simple four-quadrant box that helps you decide on and prioritize tasks by categorizing them as urgent, important, both, or neither. The quadrants are:

1. Urgent and Important (Do first): Tasks that require immediate attention are aligned with long-term goals and missions.

2. Important but Not Urgent (Schedule): Tasks that are important to your success must be planned for but do not require immediate action.

3. Urgent but Not Important (Delegate): Tasks that require immediate attention but do not contribute significantly to long-term goals.

4. Neither Urgent nor Important (Eliminate): Activities that offer no value and should be minimized or eliminated.

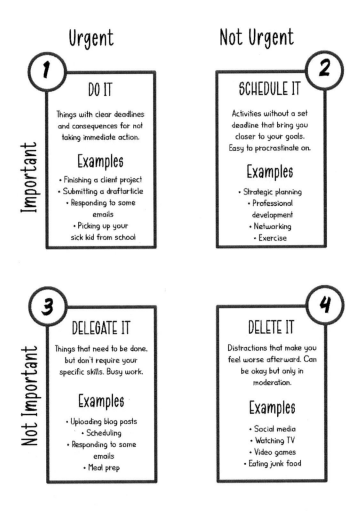

Diagram: The Eisenhower Matrix helps organize priorities, optimizing productivity.

The Matrix Revisited

In a world where everything feels urgent, it's essential to revisit this matrix with a critical eye. A contemporary approach to the Eisenhower Matrix involves an added layer of reflection and adaptability.

1. Dynamic Prioritization: In the digital age, priorities can change rapidly. Reassess your quadrants regularly to ensure they reflect the current landscape of your personal and professional life.

2. Emotional Urgency vs. Logical Urgency: Modern workers often confuse emotional urgency (a task feels urgent) with logical urgency (a task is critical to our objectives). Distinguishing between the two can save time and prevent burnout.

3. Leveraging Technology for Scheduling: For tasks in the second quadrant, use digital calendars and reminder apps to schedule focused time, ensuring these important tasks are not overlooked.

4. Delegation in the Gig Economy: Delegation isn't just for those with direct reports. Outsourcing tasks to freelancers and virtual assistants can effectively handle urgent but not important tasks.

5. Mindfulness in Elimination: The last quadrant requires ruthlessness to eliminate time-wasters. This could mean turning off unnecessary notifications, limiting time on social media, or saying no to meetings without a clear agenda.

The Role of Reflection in Prioritization

Reflection is the unsung hero in the Eisenhower Matrix. Reflecting on why a task is important can often reduce the false urgency we attach to it. Take time to understand the impact of a task and its alignment with your goals. This practice clarifies what is truly important and helps you become more comfortable with not responding to merely urgent tasks.

The Matrix and Work-Life Balance

Balancing work and personal life is challenging in the age of constant connectivity and remote work. The Eisenhower Matrix can be a valuable tool for maintaining this balance by ensuring that not all your energy is spent on "Urgent-Important" tasks. Carve out time for quadrant two, which often includes personal development, family time, and self-care—critical aspects for long-term well-being. Another way of viewing it might be that self-care tasks actually are Urgent-Important tasks, because, without them, your mental health suffers and takes your productivity down with it.

Revisiting the Eisenhower Matrix involves an evolution from a static to a dynamic tool, adaptable to the intricacies of modern life. It means applying deeper thought to what truly deserves your time. By mastering this method, you develop not just a schedule but a philosophy for life that emphasizes doing the right things instead of doing more things. In this refreshed perspective, the Eisenhower Matrix is about prioritization and cultivating the discernment to invest your most finite resource—time—into what matters most.

Part 2 The Art of Saying "No": Setting Boundaries

For many, the reluctance to say "no" stems from a fear of missing out, a desire to be liked, or an innate urge to help others. These natural inclinations make the word "no" feel like a barrier to opportunity, connection, and altruism. However, this difficulty is often at the root of time anxiety, as it can lead to a cluttered schedule, diminished personal time, and, ultimately, a sense of loss of control over one's life.

The Benefits of Saying "No"

The act of saying "no" is powerful; it is an affirmation of your own needs and priorities. It provides the space to focus on tasks and activities that align with your values and goals. More than that, it offers the opportunity to engage more fully with the tasks you do choose to take on, ensuring you can give them the attention and effort they deserve. Saying "no" is actually an act of self-care that preserves your ability to be productive, both now and in the future. Respecting your own boundaries is a responsible thing to do.

When you start saying "no," something remarkable happens. Others begin to respect your time more. This ripple effect can lead to a healthier work environment, more balanced relationships, and an overall improvement in time management and personal satisfaction.

Setting Boundaries

Saying "no" is an essential part of setting boundaries. Boundaries protect your time, energy, and emotional well-being. They help you to define what you are comfortable with and how you wish to interact with the world. Whether it's declining extra work, resisting the pull of social media, or choosing not to engage in energy-draining activities, setting boundaries is about respecting your limits.

Saying "No" to the Unimportant

The Eisenhower Matrix can guide your decision to say "no." By categorizing tasks based on urgency and importance, it becomes clearer which tasks warrant a "yes" and which should be met with a polite but firm "no." It's also about prioritizing tasks that fall into the Important but Not Urgent category—those that contribute to your long-term goals and personal growth—over those that do not.

Techniques for Saying "No" Gracefully

Saying "no" does not have to be aggressive or negative. It can be done respectfully and positively. Providing a brief explanation, offering an alternative, or simply expressing gratitude for the offer before declining are all ways to soften the blow and maintain good relationships.

"No" as a Complete Sentence

While providing context when declining a request is often helpful, it's also important to recognize that "No." is a complete sentence. You are not obliged to justify or explain your reasons if you are not comfortable doing so. This can be particularly relevant when dealing with requests that infringe on personal boundaries or values.

Saying "No" to Yourself

Sometimes, you need to say "no" to yourself. Self-imposed pressures to perform, achieve, or participate in every opportunity can be just as taxing as external requests. Learning to say "no" can mean declining to chase perfection, foregoing unnecessary commitments, or recognizing when rest is more valuable than productivity.

"No" as a Path to "Yes"

Ultimately, every "no" can be viewed as saying "yes" to something else—more time with family, space for self-care, the opportunity to work on personal projects, or simply the chance to recharge. When you close one door, it makes space for other doors or windows to appear, with new opportunities. By closing the door on less important tasks, you are creating increased space for important life-advancing opportunities. It is also about consciously prioritizing activities that bring joy, fulfillment, and balance.

In mastering the art of saying "no," one finds the path to a more intentional and contented life. It allows for the cultivation of a personal and professional existence that is not just reactive to the demands of others but is actively shaped by one's desires and needs. With each "no," you reaffirm the value of your time and the importance of your priorities—setting the stage for a life rich with time affluence and devoid of unnecessary time anxiety.

Part 3 Identifying and Focusing on High-Value Activities

Identifying and focusing on high-value activities is an essential strategy for anyone looking to optimize their time management and achieve greater results in both their personal and professional lives. When executed, these activities are the key inputs that contribute significantly to our most important goals and overall sense of fulfillment. Distinguishing and dedicating time to these tasks is critical to overcoming the pervasive feeling of time scarcity and the anxiety it breeds.

Understanding High-Value Activities

High-value activities directly correlate with our primary goals and deeply held values. They differ from low-value activities, which may appear urgent but do not substantially contribute to our long-term objectives. High-value tasks typically require significant attention and concentrated effort, often drawing upon our highest capacities for creativity and critical thinking skills. Low-value tasks are often identifiable by their low order thinking requirements and are essentially "busywork." You know it's busy-work if not much would change if you didn't do it.

Identification Process

Identifying high-value activities necessitates a reflective and honest evaluation of one's goals and how daily actions align with achieving these objectives. Tools like the Eisenhower Matrix can be instrumental in this process, enabling us to categorize tasks based on urgency and importance. High-value activities often fall into the Important but Not Urgent quadrant.

Measuring the Value of Tasks

Tasks aren't created equal; some have a much higher return on the time invested than others. A high-value task could bring in new business, enhance key skills, deepen relationships, or create future opportunities. Quantifying the value involves assessing the potential long-term impact of the activity. The question, "What will be the positive outcomes of this task in a year?" helps gauge the true value of a task.

Prioritization and Execution

After identifying high-value tasks, the next step is to ensure they take precedence in one's schedule. This may involve time blocking, where specific time slots are allocated to these activities during peak productivity periods. Conversely, it's important to eliminate or delegate low-value tasks that do not advance significant goals.

Navigating Barriers

Obstacles to focusing on high-value activities can manifest in two ways. These can be external, such as interruptions from colleagues, friends, or family, or internal resistances, such as procrastination or a reluctance to engage with complex tasks. Overcoming these obstacles might involve setting more explicit boundaries, streamlining the work environment to reduce distractions, or employing focus techniques like the Pomodoro Technique.

Leverage through Delegation and Automation

Importantly, it's not essential that you personally undertake high-value tasks if they can be efficiently delegated or automated. By assigning less critical tasks to others or using technology for repetitive jobs, more time can be allocated to activities that necessitate one's unique skills and add the most value. This represents a subcategory of high-value tasks, where you assess whether the task will be done just as well by someone or something else with minimal input from you, or whether delegation jeopardizes quality.

Investment in Learning

Spending time on personal growth and learning is often a high-value investment. Education not only enriches personal life but also broadens professional capabilities. Allocating regular intervals for growth ensures that the benefits of new knowledge and skills provide compounded returns in terms of opportunities and enhanced capabilities. This, of course, cannot be done by anyone else so delegating essential tasks that do not advance your development can leave more room for your own professional and personal growth. Just as the heading suggests, this is ultimately an investment that pays dividends.

Periodic Review and Realignment

The significance of activities can change as goals are met or evolve. It's vital to routinely reassess what constitutes high-value activities and adjust focus and resources accordingly. Things change, so a perpetual state of agility ensures that efforts are always aligned with the most impactful areas.

The Compounding Benefit

Concentrating on high-value activities results in a compounding benefit. Like compound interest in finance, the continuous investment of time in strategic areas yields an exponential return increase, propelling us toward our goals at an accelerated pace.

Maintaining Balance

While high-value activities are critical for advancement, it's also necessary to balance them with time for rest, family, and recreation, as these are also high-value in terms of overall life satisfaction. This balance is vital to avoid burnout and ensures that full energy and passion are available to engage in high-value tasks.

Embracing a focus on high-value activities transcends conventional time management advice. It's a philosophy that espouses the prioritization of impactful endeavors above all. By channeling efforts into these pivotal tasks, individuals can experience profound achievements and contentment, counteracting the effects of time anxiety with a sense of time affluence and control. The key is to work harder and smarter by identifying and executing tasks that matter most, thus crafting a personal life culture of efficacy and success.

Understanding High-Value Activities

High-value activities directly correlate with our primary goals and deeply held values. They differ from low-value activities, which may appear urgent but do not substantially contribute to our long-term objectives. High-value tasks typically require significant attention and concentrated effort, often drawing upon our highest capacities for creativity and critical thinking capacities.

Identification Process Revisited

Identifying high-value activities requires intense reflective practice. We must honestly evaluate our goals and how closely our daily actions align with achieving these objectives. Tools like the Eisenhower Matrix can be instrumental in this process, enabling us to categorize tasks based on urgency and importance, with high-value activities often falling into the Important but Not Urgent quadrant. These activities take a longer-term view.

They include new business ventures and self-improvement through personal and professional development. They are easy to push to one side when Important-Urgent tasks are baying for attention, but, ultimately, it is these high-value, self-progressing activities which will set us free. Once you have a handle on which activities are high value, it's time to apply them to their own elevated matrix of prioritization.

Prioritizing and Ranking High-Value Activities

The same processes we discussed for broadscale task prioritization can be applied to the subset of high-value tasks. After identifying high-value tasks, the next step is to ensure they take precedence in your schedule. This requires rigorous time blocking, where specific time slots are allocated to these activities during peak productivity periods. Remember that any task in the Important-Urgent category that can be delegated to technology or someone else should be.

This might be as simple as outsourcing mundane necessaries or as complex as taking the time to train someone in something that takes a lot of your time, is urgent, but is low yield. These sorts of decisions are likely to meet external and internal resistance, but all obstacles can be overcome with a sustained focus on improving your productivity and your capacity to work effectively for a life you love looking at.

Navigating Threats to Your Focus

Navigating obstacles to high-value tasks follow the same principles as any prioritization activities but the orientation is slightly different. While the motivation for resisting distractions for general important tasks might be more collective, and therefore understood by colleagues, for these high value tasks, it may only be clear to you why it's so important. Stringent timetabling and negotiated work-at-home days may assist with this challenge, or simply calling it concentration time and closing your curtains or turning your computer around.

Your internal resistance barriers require another treatment. Focusing on things that might be poorly understood by others can trigger people-pleasing urges and a sense of shame that you are focusing elsewhere. We spend such energy on the maxim "There's no I in TEAM" that self-focus can seem counter-intuitive. Let the lessons in Chapter 3 on intrinsic vs extrinsic motivation support your capacity to overcome that niggling inner voice telling you that you're focusing on the wrong thing.

And, schedule, schedule, schedule. Formalize your project time with explicit boundaries—for you and others: streamlining the work environment to reduce distractions or employing focus techniques like the Pomodoro Technique.

Part 4 The Power of Routine and Habit Stacking

Being constantly in a rush can make us overlook how consistent, small actions can bring big changes. The idea of habit stacking and having a routine is not just about organizing our day. It's actually a foundation for creating a life that's productive, meaningful, and satisfying.

The Power of Routine: Foundations of Predictability

At its essence, a routine is a set of habits that provides a framework for our daily lives. It brings a comforting predictability that can reduce stress and anxiety, as our minds are not constantly preoccupied with deciding what to do next. This predictability can free up cognitive resources for more complex tasks, enhance our focus, and improve our mental health by providing control and stability.

Anchoring the Day with Rituals

Routines often begin and end with rituals, those personal, meaningful activities that bookend our days. A morning ritual might involve meditation, exercise, or journaling, whereas an evening ritual might focus on reflection, gratitude, or planning for the next day. These rituals serve as anchors, ensuring that, regardless of the day's chaos, moments of intentional action center and prepare us for what lies ahead.

Habit Stacking: Building Complex Structures

Habit stacking, a term popularized by author S.J. Scott, takes the power of routine further by suggesting the linking of new, desired habits to established ones. By associating a new habit with an already automatic behavior, we leverage the existing neural pathways, making the new habit more likely to stick. It's about crafting a behavior sequence that flows naturally and logically, creating a complex structure from simpler building blocks.

For example, if you already drink coffee each morning, stacking a new habit of meditating for five minutes immediately after your coffee ritual can establish a new compound routine with greater ease than starting from scratch.

Creating a Compound Effect

The cumulative effect of well-structured routines and habit stacks cannot be overstated. Like interest compounding in a bank account, the benefits of consistent daily actions can compound over time, leading to significant personal and professional growth. This compound effect reinforces the value of routine and habit stacking as investment strategies for our most precious resource: time.

Strategic Habit Formation

Strategic habit formation is vital to effective habit stacking. It requires thoughtful consideration of which habits will yield the highest dividends. This might involve prioritizing habits that promote health, catalyze learning or foster relationships. By selecting habits that resonate with our long-term goals, we can ensure that our routines are aligned with our deepest values.

Overcoming the Monotony of Routine

Critics of routine often point to the monotony it can bring. Yet, the power of habit does not confine us to a life of boredom. Instead, it can create a stable foundation from which spontaneity can spring. When the minutiae of decision-making do not bog us down in every aspect of our day, we can embrace creativity and spontaneity. If you are someone who avoids routine, think about them as rhythms instead.

The world has always operated to rhythms and our bodies and minds are adapted to expect them. We have all heard that a regular waking and bedtime is beneficial, and so too is some comforting regularity to our workday. Educators and parents have long understood the power of predictable rhythms for young children, and, actually, the same can be said for all of us. The difference between us and children is that we get to set, and change, our rhythms and find the perfect sequence of habits to suit our preferences and ways of working.

Habit Stacking for Cognitive Efficiency

Habit stacking is also an exercise in cognitive efficiency. By linking habits together, we reduce the mental load of remembering to complete tasks throughout the day. (This is why little kids love them; because they are learning new things all the time.) This automation of behavior allows our brains to operate with greater efficiency, conserving mental energy for tasks that require deeper thought and creativity.

Customization and Adaptability

The beauty of routine and habit stacking is in their customization and adaptability. What works for one person may not work for another, so each individual can craft routines and habit stacks that suit their rhythms, lifestyles, and goals. And, as our lives change, so too can our routines, demonstrating an adaptable resilience that is responsive to our evolving circumstances.

The Role of Discipline

Discipline is the bedrock upon which the power of routine and habit stacking rests. This discipline enables us to stick to our routines even when motivation wanes. Discipline allows us to persevere through the initial discomfort of integrating a new habit until it becomes second nature. When this discipline is intrinsically motivated, we have the satisfaction of knowing that we are moving closer to our own goals and that we are in the driver's seat.

Routine, Reflection, and Revision

As mentioned above, an effective routine is not set in stone; it requires ongoing reflection and revision. As we grow and change, so too must our routines. This iterative process ensures that our habits always serve our current needs and aspirations, not just relics of past intentions.

In a world that often glorifies grand gestures and quick fixes, the true power lies in the quieter realm of routine and habit stacking. These are the forces that, day by seemingly insignificant day, propel us towards our goals. They do not promise overnight transformation but offer a steady, unwavering path to lasting change.

By embracing the power of routine and the art of habit stacking, we not only optimize our daily lives but also chart a course toward a future of our design. In this consistent application of small actions lies the potential for extraordinary life changes, proving that in the tapestry of life, the smallest threads, woven with intention and care, can create the richest and most enduring patterns. And, importantly, we get to set the agenda, based on things that resonate with our core life objectives.

CHAPTER 7
OVERCOMING PROCRASTINATION AND PERFECTIONISM

O vercoming procrastination and perfectionism is essential in the pursuit of effective time management and stress reduction. These two hurdles, often rooted in fear and anxiety, can cripple productivity and self-esteem. Understanding the psychological underpinnings of procrastination and perfectionism is the key to recognizing the processes in your brain, and redirecting them, before they derail your projects.

Image: Release yourself from the procrastination and perfectionism interplay!

The key is in understanding what emotions are triggering these obstructive habits. By recognizing the fears and anxieties driving these behaviors, individuals can develop strategies to address them effectively.

This involves reframing negative thoughts and beliefs, practicing self-compassion, and cultivating a growth mindset that values progress over perfection.

This part of our journey will unravel the complexities of these common barriers, providing practical techniques to break the cycle of delay and the all-or-nothing mindset. By learning to embrace imperfection and failure as opportunities for growth, rather than sources of shame, you will foster a more forgiving and productive approach to tasks and goals.

Ultimately, by balancing the desire for perfection with the pragmatism of progress, individuals can cultivate a healthier relationship with productivity, leading to increased efficiency, reduced stress, and greater overall satisfaction and fulfillment.

Part 1 Strategies to Beat Procrastination: From Planning to Action

Procrastination is a challenge that plagues many of us, hindering our productivity and often causing stress. However, with the right strategies, this common obstacle can be overcome. Here we'll explore several methods to transform planning into action and beat procrastination for good.

Understanding Procrastination

At its core, procrastination is a coping mechanism for stress and anxiety, often related to fear of failure, perfectionism, or even success. It's the gap between intention and action, where our plans become hostages to "tomorrow." To conquer procrastination, we must first dissect its causes, which are unique to each individual. Self-awareness is the first step in this strategic battle.

Conquering procrastination is a very personal process, as the root causes may vary from person to person. This is the reason that self-awareness is the first unavoidable step in the battle against procrastination. By introspectively examining our thoughts, emotions, and behaviors, we can uncover the underlying fears and anxieties that fuel our tendency to procrastinate. This self-awareness empowers us to identify patterns of avoidance and recognize the triggers that lead us down the path of procrastination.

Armed with this knowledge, we can then develop targeted strategies to overcome procrastination, tailored to our individual needs and challenges. This may involve setting realistic goals, breaking tasks into smaller, more manageable steps, and implementing techniques to mitigate the negative impact of perfectionism.

In essence, conquering procrastination requires a multifaceted approach that begins with self-awareness and extends to targeted interventions aimed at addressing the underlying causes of procrastination. In previous chapters, we have explored the intricate relationship between stress, anxiety, and procrastination.

By turning our gaze inward, we can uncover the subconscious drivers behind our unique procrastination-perfectionism dilemma. This self-awareness is pivotal in crafting a tailored approach to overcome these obstacles. Understanding our personal motivations and fears empowers us to select strategies that resonate most profoundly with our individual challenges and aspirations. With this foundation in place, we are poised to explore the following range of effective techniques designed to break the cycle of procrastination and perfectionism.

Setting Realistic Goals

Does the enormity of the task trigger procrastination for you? Setting achievable, realistic goals is crucial. Break down larger tasks into smaller, manageable parts, setting clear and specific milestones. This segmentation transforms an overwhelming project into a series of attainable steps, reducing anxiety and creating a clear roadmap from planning to action.

The Five-Minute Rule

Do you have trouble getting started on a project? One of the most effective tactics against procrastination is the five-minute rule. It's simple: Commit to doing a task for just five minutes. Often, starting is the hardest part, and once in motion, the inertia of our actions carries us forward. Five minutes can turn into an hour once we break through the initial resistance.

Time Management Techniques

Do you respond well to externalized routines and find your own self-managed projects suffering? Create your own routine structure. Effective time management is integral to overcoming procrastination. Techniques such as the Pomodoro Technique, which involves working for focused intervals followed by short breaks, can cultivate a rhythm that discourages procrastination. Scheduling tasks for your most productive times of day, known as peak times, can also maximize your efficiency.

Creating a Conducive Environment

Are you sensitive to environmental stressors? Our environment significantly influences our propensity to procrastinate. A cluttered, distraction-filled space is not conducive to focus. By curating a work environment that minimizes distractions and maximizes comfort and efficiency, we nudge ourselves towards action. This means having the necessary tools, reducing clutter, and potentially employing apps that limit our access to distractions.

Commitment Devices

Are you the kind of person who responds well to family and friends checking in on your progress? Leverage that. Commitment devices are mechanisms that help us stay accountable to our intentions. These can range from the socially mediated ones where we feel pressure to complete projects once we've shared the details with friends and family, to sophisticated apps that send us reminders, hold us to our deadlines, and even impose sanctions if we miss them (think Duolingo).

By implementing these tools, we raise the stakes of procrastination, making the act of delaying tasks less appealing and nudging us towards taking action. If pressure from others has the opposite effect on you, try something else.

Accountability Partners

This can be a good solution for those who feel the positive pressure of being part of a team. An accountability partner can serve as a powerful catalyst for action. This could be a colleague, friend, or mentor—someone who checks in on your progress and holds you responsible for your commitments. By making this relationship reciprocal, nobody feels like they are being judged or scrutinized, and the camaraderie can feel very supportive—like a workout buddy for life. Regular meetings or check-ins with this person can create a sense of obligation that propels you forward.

Reframing Thoughts

Do you catastrophize? Procrastination often stems from negative self-talk and catastrophic thinking about the task at hand. By actively reframing these thoughts into positive affirmations and realistic appraisals, we can change our emotional response to tasks. Instead of thinking, "This is impossible," we can tell ourselves, "I can take one small step."

Building on Small Wins

I think everyone responds to the power of momentum. When something good happens, don't waste it. Momentum is a powerful force. Each small task completed is a win, and these wins have a cumulative effect. They build our confidence and reinforce our perception of ourselves as people who get things done. Celebrate these wins, no matter how small, and let them propel you to the next action.

Self-Forgiveness

I'm yet to meet a procrastinator who isn't a little hard on themselves. An often-overlooked strategy is the power of self-forgiveness. Being harsh on yourself for past procrastination can fuel a negative feedback loop. Forgiving yourself can reduce the guilt that exacerbates procrastination, creating a more positive outlook that's conducive to action.

Action Planning

And planning is definitely for everyone. Action planning turns the abstract into the concrete. This involves setting a specific time and place for when and where you will perform a task. By visualizing the action in your schedule, it becomes more tangible and less likely to be pushed aside.

Combating procrastination is not about finding a one-size-fits-all solution; it's about having a variety of strategies at your disposal and knowing when to apply them. It's a skill that requires practice and patience. Through a blend of psychological insight, environmental adjustments, time management, and self-compassion, we can move from the realm of planning into the dynamic world of doing.

The transition from planning to action is a journey, but with these strategies, it's one that can be navigated successfully, leading to a life of productivity and fulfillment, free from the shackles of procrastination.

Part 2 Perfectionism: The Enemy of Done

People often think of perfectionism as a good quality, linked to being careful and aiming for the best. But when it stops you from finishing tasks and being productive, it turns into a big problem. Then, aiming for "perfect" becomes a hindrance, making it hard to just get things "done."

The Paralysis of Perfectionism

At its core, perfectionism is a relentless striving for flawlessness, an unyielding standard by which many judge themselves. This relentless pursuit can lead to a state of paralysis. Projects and tasks are started but not finished, as the perfect outcome becomes a Sisyphean task. The pursuit of perfection often results in an inability to complete tasks, leading to a backlog of work and a feeling of chronic failure.

In Greek mythology, there is a story about Sisyphus, a trickster king who was always causing Zeus trouble. A final betrayal pushed Zeus over the edge, and he sentenced him to spend an eternity in the underworld carrying an enormous boulder up a hill, only to have it roll down every time. The fate of Sisyphus can be compared to being a perfectionist. No matter how hard they try, they never feel like they have achieved the objective perfection. Sisyphus worked hard every day to haul a boulder up a mountain, but never felt the satisfaction of completing the task. This is how it feels to be a perfectionist. No matter how hard they try, their efforts never seem to be enough. The rock always rolls back down, and they feel they have to start all over again, never quite satisfied.

Sure, some perfectionists finish tasks, especially those they have to do for others. But think about how many transcripts have been published after an author's death, or how many paintings have been extracted from attics, dusted off, only to be received by the general public as works of utter perfection? Although these are extreme examples, spare a thought for Sisyphus when you're sentencing yourself to a life without task satisfaction. In his book, *The Pursuit of Perfect*, Tal Ben-Shahar issues a chilling warning. Sisyphus was sentenced to a life of toil without conquest—hauling that heavy rock was hard, but there were no rewards, because the rock just rolled down again. For perfectionists, this experience is self-inflicted. By maintaining impossible standards, they never feel the satisfaction of steadying that heavy rock at the summit and enjoying the view. As Ben-Shahar says, "There is no delight, no savoring—only another meaningless journey toward a destination that inevitably disappoints" (p.3). Perhaps one way to reduce the risk of disappointment is to avoid trying things you deeply care about; that way disappointments are contained, and the failure remains hypothetical.

This is why many perfectionists play it safe, completing only the tasks they know they can achieve, too terrified of failure to try things that truly bring them joy. They may appear accomplished at whatever parts of their psyche they are willing to "publish," but their true brilliance is confined to the proverbial attic of their fantasies, like that dusty old manuscript destined to be published posthumously.

Understanding the Root of Perfectionism

Perfectionism often stems from a fear of failure or judgment. It's a defensive strategy—one that aims to shield the perfectionist from criticism or the perceived shame of producing substandard work. To overcome perfectionism, it's essential to understand these underlying fears and address them directly.

Reframing Thoughts and Beliefs

Cognitive restructuring is a technique used in cognitive-behavioral therapy that involves identifying and challenging irrational beliefs. Perfectionists can benefit from reframing their thought patterns, such as changing "It's not good enough" to "It's good progress." By adjusting the recurring internal narrative, it's possible to diminish the power of perfectionist tendencies and allow a more realistic and self-supportive narrative to emerge.

Setting Realistic Standards

One practical step towards overcoming perfectionism is setting more realistic standards. This doesn't mean settling for mediocrity but defining what "good enough" looks like for various tasks and understanding that not all tasks require the same scrutiny and quality.

Embracing a Growth Mindset

Shifting your perspective on growth, success, and failure can be transformative for perfectionists. Perfectionists often operate with a fixed mindset, believing their abilities are static. Adopting a growth mindset encourages seeing abilities as capable of development through dedication and hard work. Embracing this mindset allows individuals to value growth over flawless performance and see mistakes as opportunities for learning rather than signs of incompetence.

The Cost of Perfectionism

The cost of perfectionism isn't just measured in unfinished tasks; it also takes a toll on mental and emotional well-being. Chronic stress, anxiety, and even depression can stem from the constant pressure perfectionists place on themselves. Moreover, it can stifle creativity, as the fear of failure inhibits risk-taking and exploration of new ideas.

Incremental Progress and Deadlines

Setting incremental goals and firm deadlines can help perfectionists to move toward completion. Deadlines force a focus on the endpoint, not just the process, compelling the perfectionist to accept the work as it is at a certain point. This approach prioritizes completion and helps to build a habit of finishing tasks.

Self-Compassion as an Antidote

Self-compassion involves treating oneself with the same kindness, concern, and support one would show a good friend. When perfectionists learn to be self-compassionate, they can alleviate some of the self-imposed pressures contributing to the procrastination and paralysis they often experience.

Prioritizing Tasks

As established, not all tasks are created equal, and perfectionists must learn to prioritize their energy and attention according to the importance of the task. By doing so, they can ensure that their perfectionism is channeled productively, where it matters most, rather than allowing it to sabotage their workflow.

The Done is Better Than Perfect Approach

The phrase "Done is better than perfect" was popularized by Sheryl Sandberg, the former COO of Facebook, in her book *Lean In*. With these words, she emphasized the importance of letting go of unattainable standards to avoid frustration and inaction. This phrase reflects a mindset that prioritizes completion and progress over the pursuit of unachievable perfection.

Perfectionism in Team Settings

In a team setting, perfectionism can slow down the individual and the collective progress. Learning to trust in colleagues' abilities and delegate can help diffuse the bottlenecks caused by perfectionism.

Celebrating Progress

Celebrate progress, no matter how imperfect. Recognizing and rewarding the completion of tasks reinforces positive behaviors and helps break the cycle of perfectionism.

While aiming for high standards is commendable, the relentless pursuit of perfection can be a significant barrier to productivity and well-being. By recognizing the pitfalls of perfectionism, redefining what success looks like, embracing imperfections, and practicing self-compassion, we can shift from a detrimental quest for the unattainable to a more productive and fulfilling work ethic that values completion and progress. Moving away from perfectionism isn't about lowering standards; it's about setting them at a human level, where "done" is not only good enough, but also exactly what was needed in the first place.

Part 3 Setting Realistic Goals and Deadlines

In a culture that glorifies constant activity and exceeding expectations, mastering the art of setting realistic objectives and sensible deadlines is crucial for our mental stability. This simple act of resistance to the unreasonable not only helps you, but also acts as a powerful model for change. It provides relief from the common problem of feeling overwhelmed by time constraints, while sending a clear message to your colleagues that you are human, and they are too.

Learning to set achievable targets can revolutionize our approach to time, ease stress, and increase our productivity. If you are in a position of authority, it can also revolutionize the workplace culture of your office. If people are setting realistic goals, they are more likely to achieve them.

This in turn supports self-esteem and a sense of achievement and combats all of the negative self-talk that can lead to heightened stress, which—as we've discussed—reduces productivity anyway. It's not about lowering standards so everyone can relax, it's about showing yourself and your colleagues the compassion and respect they deserve and allowing people to feel a sense of achievement. This next section provides details about effective and realistic goal setting, how it supports mental health, and ultimately business success.

Understanding the Significance of Realistic Goals

Realistic goals are the pitstops on the journey of life. By itemizing the elements of our loftier goals, individuals can break down their aspirations into manageable tasks and milestones. This is simply project management, whereby milestones are established and critical paths are mapped, but these principles should be applied to all personal goals as well.

This breakdown enables a clear roadmap towards the realization of dreams, providing a structured approach to navigate challenges and track progress effectively. Realistic goals serve as a compass, guiding us to make informed decisions and prioritizing tasks in alignment with our overarching core objectives. They keep us on track, focused on what truly matters, fostering a sense of purpose and motivation in pursuit of success. In essence, realistic goals transform abstract dreams into tangible realities, bridging the gap between vision and action.

They enable individuals to stay motivated and focused, providing a clear direction for their efforts. The ability to set and meet realistic goals is often a distinguishing characteristic of successful individuals.

The Psychology of Goal Setting

The psychology behind goal setting is rooted in motivation and the reward systems within our brains. Goals give us a sense of purpose, and when they are achieved, they release dopamine, making us feel good and encouraging us to continue setting and achieving goals. In Chapter 3, we discussed intrinsic and extrinsic motivation. Both give us the dopamine hit when we achieve something.

If it the motivation is extrinsic, it comes from outside and can't be controlled by us. Conversely, personalized goal setting is inherently intrinsic. You set the goal, and you achieve the goal. It's a reward of personal satisfaction, and some goal setters actually do reward themselves with a massage, holiday, or just five minutes to themselves. If and how you do this will depend on how much you value achievement itself or what you value. There's no right or wrong way. You are in charge of how you motivate yourself. There are useful and universally applicable frameworks for defining goals however, and these will suit everyone.

SMART Goals Framework

The SMART framework is a well-established tool for setting goals. Goals should be Specific, Measurable, Achievable, Relevant, and Time-bound. This framework ensures that goals are clear and reachable within a reasonable timeframe, thus increasing the likelihood of success.

Diagram: SMART Goals Framework

Specific: Business goals should be clearly defined and unambiguous. For instance, rather than setting a vague goal like "increase sales" a specific goal would be "increase monthly sales by 10%."

Measurable: It's essential to have metrics to track progress towards your goals. For example, if a company aims to improve customer satisfaction, they might measure it by the percentage of positive customer feedback received or through Net Promoter Score (NPS) surveys. Without a metric, how do we know the goal has been achieved?

Achievable: This element is closely aligned with our realistic goals discussion. Goals should be realistic and attainable given the resources and constraints available. For instance, a startup aiming to disrupt the market might set a goal to reach a certain number of users within a year, considering factors such as market demand and available funding.

Relevant: Goals should align with overall objectives and priorities, and this can apply to business or personal and professional development goals. For instance, if a company's strategic focus is on expanding into new markets, setting a goal to increase market share in existing markets might not be as relevant as setting a goal to penetrate new markets.

Time-bound: Setting a deadline creates a sense of urgency and helps to maintain focus. This closely aligns with our discussion above on the importance of chunking goals into manageable stages on the journey. This translates to points on the graph, where each point represents a goal achieved, and each goal sits within a continuum—culminating in the main goal being achieved.

Personal SMART Goals: A Clear Roadmap for Personal Achievement

Setting personal SMART goals can significantly contribute to individual success by providing a clear roadmap for personal development and achievement. Let's explore how each aspect of the SMART framework contributes to individual success:

Specific: The clarity provided by specific goals helps individuals stay focused and avoids ambiguity of purpose—enabling them to direct efforts more effectively towards achieving core life objectives.

Measurable: This one might seem tricky for a personal goal, but everything can be quantified. Establishing measurable criteria allows an objective assessment of our performance—even on personal things like rest or time with family. How many New Year revelers say, "This year, I plan to spend more time with my loved ones"? How much more time? Choose a percentage that seems reasonable. Track your activities for a month. If you've achieved it but you don't feel connected enough, adjust upwards. If you haven't achieved the percentage but all is well, you can probably reduce. This is the power of measuring personal goals.

Achievable: Setting goals that are realistic and attainable ensures that individuals are not setting themselves up for failure. Achievable goals motivate individuals to take action and maintain momentum, as they can see tangible progress towards their objectives.

Relevant: Aligning goals with personal values, interests, and long-term aspirations ensures that individuals remain motivated and engaged in pursuing them. Relevant goals resonate with individuals on a deeper level, increasing their commitment and determination to succeed. This is where you assess the legitimacy of each goal by comparing it against your core objectives for life.

Time-bound: Establishing deadlines creates a sense of accountability. It also allows for timely assessment and reassessment of achievement and next steps. Time-bound goals prevent procrastination and encourage individuals to take consistent action towards achieving their objectives.

Overall, setting SMART goals empowers us to take control of our personal and professional growth. It provides a structured approach to goal-setting that enhances clarity, motivation, and accountability. The following list of considerations are all supported by, and relevant to, SMART goals. They have been selected as a checklist for ensuring your SMART goals are working as they should, and ultimately leading to greater fulfillment and achievement in both personal and professional endeavors.

Breaking Down Large Goals

Large, long-term goals can often seem overwhelming. Breaking them into smaller, more manageable tasks can make them appear less daunting and more approachable. This also allows for regular progress checks and adjustments.

The Importance of Flexibility

While deadlines are important, it's equally crucial to remain flexible. Unforeseen circumstances can arise, and rigid adherence to deadlines may not always be possible or healthy. Being able to adjust goals and deadlines can prevent unnecessary stress and burnout.

Prioritizing Tasks

Prioritizing tasks is an essential step in goal-setting. Not all tasks are equally important, and focusing on the most critical ones ensures that time and resources are used effectively. This helps achieve the most important goals first, creating momentum for less critical tasks.

Realistic Time Estimates

One of the most common mistakes in setting deadlines is underestimating the time required to complete a task. Analyzing tasks critically and basing time estimates on past experiences or industry standards is important. Building in extra time for contingencies can also prevent a last-minute rush.

The Role of Accountability

Accountability can significantly increase the chances of achieving a goal. Sharing goals with a colleague, friend, or coach can provide an external source of motivation and a sense of obligation to meet the commitments.

Feedback Loops

Regular feedback on progress towards a goal is crucial for continuous improvement. Feedback helps identify areas that require more attention and allows for real-time adjustments to the plan.

The Art of Goal Laddering

Goal laddering involves setting a series of smaller goals leading to a larger one. This step-by-step approach can make even the most ambitious goals attainable by providing a clear pathway to success.

Revisiting and Revising Goals

Goals should not be static; they must evolve as situations change. Regularly reviewing and revising goals ensures that they remain relevant and achievable.

Celebrating Milestones

Recognizing and celebrating the achievement of milestones helps maintain motivation and can increase self-efficacy. It serves as a reminder that progress is being made, even if the ultimate goal has yet to be reached.

The Importance of Work-Life Balance

In pursuing goals, it's crucial not to overlook work-life balance. Setting goals for a healthy lifestyle will enable sustained effort over time and prevent burnout.

Time Management Techniques

Effective time management techniques such as time blocking, the Pomodoro Technique, or the Eisenhower Matrix can aid in achieving goals. They can help allocate time wisely, focus efforts, and track progress against deadlines.

Technology as an Aid

Various technological tools can assist in setting and tracking goals. Project management software, apps, and even simple spreadsheets can help visualize progress and maintain focus on deadlines.

Dealing with Setbacks

Setbacks are inevitable in any endeavor. The ability to deal with them constructively—by analyzing what went wrong, making the necessary adjustments, and moving forward—is integral to the goal-setting process.

To sum up, setting realistic goals and deadlines is a dynamic and adaptable process that requires a balance of ambition and practicality. It's about understanding limitations, anticipating challenges, and maintaining the flexibility to adapt as needed.

Realistic goals guide personal and professional growth, marking the journey from aspiration to achievement. By focusing on actionable steps, celebrating small victories, and adjusting strategies when needed, individuals can enhance their productivity and foster a sense of accomplishment and contentment in their daily lives.

Part 4 The Role of Accountability Partners and Coaches

The role of accountability partners and coaches has emerged as instrumental to success in time management and personal development. An accountability partner is someone who coaches another person in terms of helping the other person keep a commitment. These relationships can be transformative, catalyzing progress by leveraging human psychology and social dynamics. This next section explores the multifaceted roles of accountability partners and coaches, the mechanisms by which they enhance personal productivity, and the best practices for fostering effective accountability relationships.

Understanding Accountability in Time Management

In the context of time management, accountability is a commitment to meeting the goals and deadlines we set for ourselves. It involves actively holding ourselves accountable for completing tasks and goals within set time frames. Assigning an accountability partner or a coach to monitor our progress is a conscious and explicit act of intention.

Aside from the fact that the explicit intentionality of assigning a coach (or accountability partner) orientates your psyche towards your goals, external monitoring fosters a stronger sense of responsibility and often enhances productivity and concentration. In this way, you have recruited both intrinsic and extrinsic motivational forces to the task of achieving your goals.

The mechanism in the brain that creates this accountability is similar to extrinsic motivation (such as motivation that comes from external compulsion/threats/rewards). However, because you set the system in motion, the process is actually controlled by you. You can switch it on, and also switch it off. You decide who you trust to take on this role, so you can select someone who will offer constructive feedback, rather than triggering unhelpful feelings of guilt or shame.

You know what motivates you, and you can even suggest to them ahead of time what sorts of encouragements or comments to make at various intervals. We can also instruct our accountability partner on what we would like them to say to us if we miss a deadline. This external oversight heightens an individual's sense of responsibility and can lead to increased productivity and focus.

Image: Select accountability partners that you trust to help you when you need it most!

The Impact of Accountability Partners

An accountability partner works alongside you to ensure you stay on track with your goals. This partnership can be informal, such as a friend or colleague, or more formal, such as a mastermind group member or a professional mentor. The key attribute of an effective accountability partner is a shared commitment to mutual success and progress.

The Many Benefits of Accountability Partners

Motivation and Encouragement: When motivation wanes, an accountability partner provides encouragement and a reminder of the reasons behind pursuing your goals.

Objective Insight: An external party can offer unbiased feedback and observations, helping to identify blind spots or areas for improvement that might be overlooked.

Shared Resources and Knowledge: Partners often bring their own experiences and insights, which can be invaluable in overcoming obstacles and refining time management strategies.

Social Support: We are essentially social creatures, and knowing someone else is invested in your success can alleviate the loneliness that sometimes accompanies personal endeavors.

The Distinct Role of Coaches

Where an accountability partner may act as a peer, a coach typically provides a more structured and professional level of guidance. Coaches are trained to help clients develop time management skills, set realistic goals, and create actionable plans to achieve them. They utilize various tools and methodologies to facilitate progress and are adept at challenging their clients to expand their capabilities.

Advantages of Engaging a Coach

Expertise: Coaches bring specialized knowledge and techniques that can transform an individual's approach to managing time.

Tailored Strategies: Coaches are skilled in crafting personalized strategies that align with an individual's specific needs, preferences, and life circumstances.

Accountability and Follow-Through: Coaches hold clients accountable to their goals and the processes and habits that lead to those goals.

Empowerment: Good coaching empowers individuals to become self-reliant, fostering skills that are beneficial long after the coaching relationship has ended.

Strategies for Working with Accountability Partners and Coaches

Clear Communication: Establish open and honest communication from the start. Define expectations, goals, and the preferred methods of feedback.

Regular Check-Ins: Schedule consistent meetings or updates to review progress, discuss challenges, and adjust plans as necessary.

Constructive Feedback: Encourage a feedback loop that is constructive and focused on actionable insights rather than criticism.

Mutual Respect: Build a relationship founded on mutual respect and trust, ensuring both parties feel valued and heard.

Commitment to Action: Move beyond planning and discussing by committing to specific actions following each accountability session.

Celebration of Success: Acknowledge and celebrate successes to build momentum and reinforce the value of the accountability structure.

Maximizing the Effectiveness of Accountability Relationships

To make the most of an accountability relationship, one must be prepared to act upon the advice and feedback received. It involves a willingness to step out of comfort zones and implement changes that may at times feel challenging. Additionally, it is crucial to remain flexible and adaptable, as the journey toward better time management is often non-linear and requires continuous learning and adjustment.

Overcoming Reluctance to Seek Support

Individuals often hesitate to seek accountability partners or coaches due to pride, fear of vulnerability, or a belief that they should manage independently. Overcoming this reluctance is pivotal as it opens the door to collaboration and support that can drastically improve time management capabilities.

The role of accountability partners and coaches in managing time, particularly for those affected by time anxiety, is invaluable. These relationships offer structure, support, and expertise that foster an environment conducive to growth and improvement. Accountability in time management is not just about adherence to goals; it is about embarking on a collaborative journey toward self-improvement, embracing the collective experience, and leveraging external insights for personal advancement.

It is about the transformational realization that sometimes, the best way to multiply time is to collaborate with others who are invested in your success and can help you make the most of the time you have. Ultimately, the synergy created through accountability can turn the elusive sands of time into a solid foundation upon which enduring habits, efficiency, and personal satisfaction are built.

CHAPTER 8
CREATING YOUR PERSONALIZED PLAN

Starting the process of overcoming time anxiety involves gaining new understandings and adopting practical actions that come together in a personalized plan for managing your time. This final chapter will take you through an eight-step method to develop a plan that suits you specifically. Each step in this process is designed to help you better understand your relationship with time, identify what causes you stress, and learn how to deal with these challenges effectively. By the end of this final chapter, you will have a clear, customized strategy to manage your time more efficiently, reduce your anxiety, and improve your overall well-being and productivity in both your personal and professional life.

Part 1 Step-by-Step Guide to Developing Your Plan

This 8-Step Guide provides a clear and structured approach to creating a time management plan tailored to your needs. It's more than just a list of tasks; it's a transformative strategy for your lifestyle. Your plan needs to be customized to fit your personal and professional life seamlessly, enabling you to navigate each day with confidence and purpose, free from the constraints of time anxiety.

First, you need to identify the unique factors that contribute to your time anxiety and develop practical steps to address them. By focusing on your specific challenges and goals, the plan encourages a more mindful and efficient use of time. It aims to empower you with the skills to prioritize tasks effectively, set achievable goals, and establish a balanced schedule that accommodates work responsibilities, personal interests, and relaxation.

Image: What's your perfect recipe for a time management plan?

As you implement this plan, you'll notice an enhanced sense of control and confidence in how you manage your time. This newfound mastery over your schedule will help alleviate the stress and anxiety associated with time management, allowing you to move through your days more purposefully and easily. The end goal is a more harmonious and productive lifestyle, free from the pressures and constraints of time anxiety, enabling you to enjoy a more fulfilling personal and professional life.

1. Self-Assessment: Identify Your Time-Anxiety Profile

Before you can manage time anxiety, you need to understand its roots. Begin deep diving into your daily routines, noting when anxiety peaks. Is it during the morning rush, end-of-day deadlines, or Sunday evenings? Identifying these patterns is the first critical step toward building your personalized plan.

Keep a journal for at least a week to see patterns emerge over the full range of rest and workdays. Make sure you select a "typical" week, so you get the best idea of the norms in your life. Record not just what you do but how you feel about it, as this will give you insight into the activities that cause the most stress.

2. Establish Clear Goals: Define What Time Affluence Means to You

What does a well-managed day look like in your world? Define what "time affluence" means to you. How this looks will vary from person to person. It might be having an hour of uninterrupted family time or space for creative projects. Your goals should reflect what you value most, serving as your plan's cornerstone. Remember that affluence of any kind is only as valuable as what you spend it on. This goes for time too.

When establishing your goals, be SMART (Specific, Measurable, Achievable, Relevant, Time-bound). This framework ensures your goals are well-defined and attainable within a specific timeframe.

3. Prioritize: Create a Hierarchy of Tasks and Commitments

Not all tasks are created equal. Categorize your responsibilities based on urgency and importance. Utilize tools like the Eisenhower Matrix to help you prioritize effectively. This will streamline your workflow and provide insights as to where your time is best invested.

In prioritization, it's important to distinguish between tasks that require your unique skills and those that can be delegated or postponed. Remember, saying "yes" to everything is the same as saying "no" to your priorities.

4. Adopt Time-Management Techniques: Find Tools That Resonate

Experiment with various time management methods, from the Pomodoro Technique to time blocking. The aim is to find what resonates with your work style and stick to it. Remember, consistency is key to making any time management technique work.

Flexibility is vital in time-management techniques. If you're a morning person, tackle high-priority tasks when your energy is highest. If you're a night owl, reserve evenings for deep work. Aligning tasks with your natural rhythms can enhance efficiency and reduce stress.

5. Address Procrastination and Perfectionism: Tackle the Time Thieves

Procrastination and perfectionism can exacerbate time anxiety. Address these directly by setting realistic deadlines and breaking tasks into smaller, manageable steps. Accept that "perfect" is often the enemy of "done" and aim for progress, not perfection.

Confronting procrastination and perfectionism may involve psychological shifts. Challenge irrational beliefs about the need to be perfect and confront fears of failure that often fuel procrastination.

6. Set Boundaries: Learn the Art of Saying "No"

Creating buffers against time stealers is crucial. Learn to say "no" to non-essential tasks and avoid overcommitting. This also means setting boundaries with others, protecting your time as your most valuable resource.

Setting boundaries will likely involve difficult conversations and internal adjustments. Be clear on your limits and communicate them with kindness and firmness.

7. Incorporate Self-Care: Balance Productivity with Well-being

Your plan should include self-care routines. Whether it's a daily walk, meditation, or a hobby, ensure these are scheduled into your day. They aren't just breaks but recharging stations for your mind and body, essential for sustainable productivity. These activities should be just as much part of the plan as your work.

The temptation with self-care might be to see these activities as optional. Instead, view them as critical elements of your plan. Neglecting self-care can lead to burnout, which is counterproductive to managing time effectively.

8. Reflect and Adjust: Regularly Review Your Plan

Finally, set aside time each week to reflect on what's working and what isn't. Your plan isn't set in stone; it's a living document that should evolve as you do. Don't be afraid to adjust techniques, swap tools, or reprioritize tasks to fit your current circumstances better.

In your reflection and adjustment, utilize quantitative data (how much you achieved) and qualitative insights (how you felt). This holistic review allows you to effectively recalibrate your approach to managing time and anxiety.

Following the steps in this book will help you prioritize tasks, set realistic goals, and create a balanced schedule that includes time for work, rest, and play. It will also teach you how to be more present and mindful, so you're not constantly worrying about the past or future.

The core purpose of this approach is to give you a sense of control over your time, allowing you to use it in a way that aligns with your values and goals. By implementing these strategies, you'll find that time becomes a resource you can manage and enjoy rather than a source of constant stress.

Part 2 How to Adjust When Life Throws Curveballs

Curveballs are an inevitable part of life, but with the right mindset and approach, they can be managed and even leveraged for personal development. Adjusting to life's curveballs is essential for maintaining resilience and mental well-being in case of unexpected changes and challenges. In Part 1, we developed your plan, along with strategies for continuous assessment of goals and progress. Part 2 offers a guide to staying afloat and adjusting when life events threaten to throw you off course.

Remember, resilience is not just about bouncing back; it's about bouncing forward, using the experience to propel you into a future that may be different from what you envisioned but is rich with possibility. Each step you take, from the initial response to the strategic planning and ongoing self-care, builds your resilience and prepares you for whatever comes next.

Understand and Accept Change

Life is unpredictable. Acceptance is the first step in adapting to any curveball. Recognize that change is an inevitable part of life and that some factors are beyond your control. Give yourself permission to feel upset or stressed, but also remind yourself that your reaction to the change is something you can control.

Identify the Impact

When a curveball comes your way, take a moment to assess its immediate impact. What are the tangible effects on your daily routine, responsibilities, and goals? Identifying these will help you understand the scope of the adjustment needed.

Reassess Priorities

In light of the new situation, your priorities may need to shift. What was important yesterday may not be as critical today. Reevaluate your priorities based on the new circumstances and focus on what's most important to maintain stability.

Develop a Flexible Mindset

Cultivating a flexible mindset is key to adjusting to change. It involves being open to new ways of thinking and acting. View the situation from different angles and be willing to try out new solutions.

Set Realistic Expectations

Set realistic expectations for yourself during this period of adjustment. Understand that it might take time to find your footing once more, and you may not be as productive as usual while this is happening. Be kind to yourself and set achievable goals.

Create a New Plan

With new priorities and a flexible mindset, you can start creating a plan to deal with the change. Break down the plan into small, manageable steps that you can follow sequentially when you need to begin adjusting to the new situation.

Build a Support Network

Reach out to friends, family, or professionals who can offer support. Sharing your concerns with others can provide relief and may lead to practical solutions you hadn't considered.

Maintain Routine Where Possible

Even though some aspects of your life are changing, maintaining certain routines can provide a sense of stability. Keep up with regular activities that are not impacted by the change to give your day structure.

Learn and Adapt

As you implement your new plan, note what works and what doesn't. Be prepared to learn from the experience and adapt your approach as necessary.

Look After Your Well-being

Ensure that you care for your physical and emotional health. Exercise, proper nutrition, sufficient sleep, and mindfulness practices can all contribute to a better capacity to cope with stress. Consciously planning for these needs to be met is a crucial part of any successful life plan.

Embrace Personal Growth

Every challenge presents an opportunity for personal growth. Reflect on what you can learn from the experience and how it can contribute to your development. Using this learning is vital for continual movement toward our most fundamental life goals.

Stay Positive and Forward-Looking

Try to maintain a positive outlook. Focus on potential opportunities from the situation rather than dwelling on what has been lost or disrupted.

Adjusting to life's curveballs requires time, patience, and the willingness to adapt. You can navigate through uncertainty by accepting change, reassessing your priorities, and creating a flexible plan of action. Remember to lean on your support network and take care of your well-being as you adapt. With a positive and growth-oriented mindset, you can turn challenges into opportunities for personal development and find new paths to success.

Part 3 Balancing Flexibility and Structure

In a world that is constantly changing, the art of balancing flexibility with structure is not just useful but necessary. While structure gives us a framework to organize our lives and activities, flexibility allows us to adapt to the unforeseen and embrace the flow of life's ever-changing circumstances. Mastering the equilibrium between these two can improve mental health, increase productivity, and achieve a more satisfying personal life.

Flexibility vs. Structure: Understanding the Spectrum

Flexibility and structure are often seen as opposing forces, but they exist on a spectrum. Too much structure can lead to rigidity, while too much flexibility can lead to chaos. The goal is to find a harmonious balance where both benefits can be realized.

The Benefits of Structure

Structure provides a sense of order and predictability. You might like to think of this firm structure like a tree; the external environment influences where a tree grows a new branch, how thick it grows, and how plentiful the foliage.

The strong trunk provides the stability and reliability needed for the tree's creative output. This strong base can improve efficiency and support the creative output. A baseline routine is a structured approach to your day that can lead to a more disciplined life, reducing the need for constant decision-making.

The Power of Flexibility

On the other hand, flexibility provides the range of movement that allows you to bend without breaking. It's the ability to adapt to new information, unexpected events, and life's inevitable changes. Flexibility can foster creativity and resilience and can lead to better problem-solving.

Finding Your Balance

Self-Assessment: Start by assessing your natural inclination. Do you crave order or thrive in a more fluid environment? Your tendencies will influence your balancing act.

Prioritize: Understand what needs structure in your life and what can benefit from flexibility. Priorities such as work deadlines might require a strict schedule, while personal hobbies may allow for a more relaxed approach.

Create Routines: Establish routines for the non-negotiables. Morning rituals, work schedules, and exercise routines can provide the structure needed to ensure these tasks are completed efficiently.

Plan for the Unplanned: Build buffers for unexpected tasks or opportunities in your schedule. Allowing time blocks in your day for the unforeseen means you can adapt without disrupting your entire routine.

Set Goals but Adapt Strategies: Have clear goals but be open to changing your strategies to achieve them. The endpoint remains fixed, but the path there can vary.

Embrace Change: When change occurs, view it as an opportunity rather than an obstacle. Flexibility in mindset leads to a more proactive and less reactive life.

Learn to Say "No": Understand that being flexible doesn't mean saying "yes" to everything. Being selective means you can be flexible with the commitments you choose to take on, and you conserve time for core goals.

Reflect Regularly: Take time to reflect on how your balance is working.

What adjustments need to be made? Has there been a shift in priorities that requires a different approach? How have you been feeling about your productivity? Your goals?

Implementing a Balanced Approach

Time Management: Use tools like time-blocking to structure your day but remain flexible enough to move blocks around as needed.

Task Management: Utilize lists for tasks that require structure and deadlines, but also maintain a separate list for tasks that have flexibility in when and how they are completed.

Communication: Communicate with those around you about your need for both structure and flexibility. Setting expectations can help others understand and support your balance.

Mindset: Develop a growth mindset that sees the value in both planning and adapting. Avoid an all-or-nothing mentality, which can lead to frustration.

Contingency Planning: Always have a Plan B. Having an alternative can prevent stress if something in your structured plan doesn't work out.

Striking the Balance in Different Life Areas

Work: You may have to adhere to a structured schedule but be flexible in accomplishing tasks, collaborating with others, and meeting deadlines.

Personal Life: Your personal life may offer more opportunities for flexibility. Be structured with important personal goals but flexible in your leisure activities.

Relationships: Relationships benefit from a structured commitment to time together but require flexibility in handling conflicts and differences of opinion and supporting each other through changes.

Health: Follow a structured health and wellness routine but be flexible. If you miss a workout, find a way to incorporate physical activity differently that day.

Balancing flexibility and structure is a dynamic, deeply personal, and constantly evolving process. It's not about choosing one over the other but integrating both into your life for a holistic approach to living. By embracing the strengths of structure and flexibility, you position yourself to cope with life's demands and thrive amidst them. Remember that balance is not a one-time achievement but a continual adjustment, much like the act of balancing itself.

Part 4 Setting Up for a Time-Affluent Future

Embarking on the path to a time-affluent future involves redefining your concept of wealth to prioritize time as much as money or material success. Achieving time affluence is about having enough time to engage in personally fulfilling and meaningful activities. It's not just about having free time, but about having the freedom to choose how you spend that time.

In this approach, the focus shifts from accumulating material wealth to creating a balanced life where time is a precious and well-utilized resource. This doesn't necessarily mean having vast amounts of leisure time; rather, it's about the quality and fulfillment you derive from how you spend your time. Time affluence allows you to experience life more deeply and richly, enabling you to be present in the moment and engage fully with the world around you.

As you strive for time affluence, you learn to prioritize and make conscious choices about how you allocate your time, aligning your daily activities with your core values and long-term goals. This might involve setting boundaries at work, simplifying your lifestyle, or redefining success in a way that values personal growth and happiness over traditional markers of success. The ultimate aim is to lead a life where time is spent meaningfully, contributing to a sense of fulfillment, balance, and contentment.

Embracing a New Metric for Success

The pursuit of time affluence requires a paradigm shift in how we measure success. While this is by no means universal, success in most dominant cultural paradigms is gauged by career achievements or material accumulation. Conversely, a time-affluence worldview places more value on the freedom and autonomy to spend time as one chooses. The shift begins with an individual reassessment of what constitutes a rich and fulfilling life.

Prioritizing Time Over Money

Choosing time over money is a foundational decision in becoming time affluent. This doesn't dismiss the importance of financial stability but emphasizes that incremental increases in income often have diminishing returns on well-being. Instead, it advocates for a balance where earning is aligned with time to pursue passions, relax, and be with loved ones.

It's also not a zero-sum situation. Often, when we set aside time to focus on things that truly resonate with us, success follows us. A famous quote by philosopher and motivational speaker Alan Watts springs to mind. When Dr. Watts advised university students on career development, he would start with a simple question: What do you desire? He would ask them, "What makes you itch?"

When he finally got them to identify their core desire, he would say, "You do that and forget the money." He told them that if they really loved it, they would become a master, and the money would come. He also told them this: "The only way to become a master of something is to be really with it." Being really "with it" means being present with it, totally focused on it and this can only happen when we are aligned with our core life goals. So how can you focus on what you truly desire?

Delegation and Outsourcing

To create more personal time, delegating tasks that are time-consuming and offer little personal satisfaction or growth is essential. This can mean outsourcing household chores, using technology to automate tasks, or hiring professionals. Delegating effectively multiplies your time and allows you to focus on high-value activities. Placing value on your own time immediately makes it a quantifiable resource. Would you pay someone what you think you're worth to do a certain task? If not, delegate, and pay someone what it's worth to do it for you.

Investing in Time-Saving Resources

Investing in resources that save time can be as important as financial investments. Whether it's buying appliances that reduce daily chores or paying for services that free up weekends, the return on investment is measured in time gained for more fulfilling activities.

Time-First Decision Making

Making decisions with a time-affluent mindset involves considering the time implications of any new commitment. Before taking on a new project or purchase, ask how it will affect your time. Will it bring joy and satisfaction, or will it become another time-consuming obligation?

Boundary Setting for Time Protection

Boundaries are essential in safeguarding your time. This means learning to say "no" to requests that don't align with your priorities, setting limits on work hours, and ensuring leisure time is respected and uninterrupted.

Creating Efficient Systems

Efficiency isn't just for the workplace. Creating systems in your personal life for tasks like shopping, meal prep, and household management can reduce the time spent on necessary but low-satisfaction tasks, increasing overall time affluence.

Planning for Time-Rich Experiences

Time affluence is about creating space for experiences that enrich life. This involves intentionally planning vacations, hobbies, and downtime. It's also about leaving space for spontaneity, the unexpected opportunities that often lead to the most memorable moments.

Mindful Consumption

A time-affluent future also involves mindful consumption, recognizing that every purchase has a time cost associated with it, whether it's maintenance, management, or the work required to afford it. By being more selective with consumption, you can reduce these hidden time costs.

Career Choices

Professions and employers vary greatly in how they impact time affluence. Seeking roles that offer flexibility, valuing leisure time ahead of paid overtime, and working for organizations that support work-life balance can greatly increase time wealth.

Education and Continuous Learning

Investing in education and learning can lead to greater time affluence by opening up opportunities for more satisfying and flexible work. Lifelong learning ensures adaptability in a changing job market, potentially leading to more time-friendly career paths. Learning is also expansive for the mind and lays down new neural pathways that cultivate new ways of thinking and changed perspectives.

Building a Time-Affluent Community

The pursuit of time affluence isn't just individual; it's also about fostering communities that value time over material wealth. This can involve supporting local businesses, engaging in community activities, and advocating for policies that promote work-life balance.

Health as a Time Investment

Good health is essential for a time-affluent future. Investing time in exercise, sleep, and healthy eating pays dividends in terms of energy and longevity, enabling a fuller and more engaged life.

Financial Planning for Time Affluence

Financial planning with a focus on time affluence may involve different strategies, like early retirement planning, investing in passive income streams, or saving for sabbaticals. This financial security provides the freedom to make time-based decisions without undue stress.

Teaching Time Management to Next Generations

Fostering a culture of time affluence includes educating children about time management and the value of free time. Encouraging younger generations to appreciate and manage time well ensures the perpetuation of time-affluent values.

A Resilient Approach to Life's Uncertainties

A time-affluent future is also a resilient one. By valuing time and the freedom it brings, individuals are better equipped to deal with life's uncertainties. Time affluence provides the space to adapt to changes, whether they're personal, professional, or global.

Building a future that treasures time affluence is a comprehensive endeavor. It encompasses personal values, daily habits, financial planning, and societal engagement. It is about constructing a life that affords you the time to engage deeply with the world around you, pursue growth and learning, and experience joy and contentment. The journey to time affluence is about redefining wealth to include the richness of experiences, relationships, and personal fulfillment that only time can buy.

IN CONCLUSION:
BE HERE NOW

In the pages of this book, we have explored the complex topic of time anxiety, exploring its psychological and physiological roots, as well as its impact on our lives. We explored the philosophy of time management, challenged traditional notions of productivity, and shifted our time paradigm from an obsession with long hours of meaningless toil to impactful allocation of our most precious resource: time.

We have explored adopting a culture of time affluence, where your time is precious, and you live each moment with mindfulness and presence in the moment. By committing to single-tasking and prioritization of your core desires, you are your own master, with practical tools and techniques, such as time blocking, mindfulness, and technology to support you in managing time anxiety effectively.

In these pages, you have also learnt the mastery of prioritization, and how to overcome the procrastination and perfectionism interplay as you create your personalized plans for managing time effectively.

It is likely that your reflective journey to temporal emancipation has begun. With an assessment of your own time-anxiety profile underway, you have—by now, I imagine—identified at least some of your time anxiety triggers. You may have begun evaluating your habits and coping mechanisms.

You may even have begun to develop strategies and plans to transform your thinking from a quantity-based model to a quality-based time management orientation.

Or perhaps you have simply read the book, and stayed wholly in the moment, really present with it, with only your self-reflective inner monologue as your companion. Whichever way you have chosen to use this book will be what's right for you. And it will always be here for you to remind you of the vital aspects of taking control of your time.

If you find yourself glancing at the clock and feeling that tightness in your chest and panic take hold, you know how to unravel the tension and reflect, analyze, plan, and transform your way back to a healthy relationship with time.

So, take control. Live fully. Remember, really living is not about racing through moments; it's about finding peace by embracing the spaces between.

ABOUT THE AUTHOR

Sarah is a seasoned business leader with over three decades of experience spanning diverse industries and continents. Born in Gibraltar, she embarked on a global journey that led her from the UK to Australia, Japan, and Dubai in the Middle East.

Her professional odyssey began in merchant banking before transitioning through fashion buying and multimedia events, ultimately finding her niche in the advertising space of creative and digital production. With a career dedicated to managing large cross-functional teams, Sarah understands the feeling that life can feel like life has become nothing more than a series of deadlines, milestones, and completions. She spent decades of her life rushing from deadline to deadline, punctuated by equally hectic vacations.

Beyond her professional life, Sarah is a certified Life and Retirement Coach, driven by her passion for empowering others to embrace authenticity and live boldly. Drawing from her own journey, Sarah offers guidance infused with real-world wisdom and a touch of joy.

A lifelong learner and avid reader of self-help literature, Sarah's latest endeavor culminates in this book, Time Management for the Time-Anxious, where she shares insights garnered from personal struggles and triumphs. She hopes that by sharing her experience of years of time anxiety and lessons learnt will save you from your own missed opportunities and get you well on your way to living life in the moment.

A true author of multi-age appeal, Sarah also shares insights from a childhood full of new beginnings in her range of children's books about the same struggles and triumphs—just on a smaller scale. Through her writing, mentoring, and coaching, Sarah aspires to serve as a source of support and guidance, enriching the lives of her readers one insightful chat at a time.

Join our Mailing List

Scan the QR code below to sign up to our Newsletter mailing list and receive your free bonus gift.

Our newsletters are full of valuable insights and helpful tips on productivity and mastering time management. We promise to deliver quality content that's both informative and inspiring, without overwhelming your inbox with unnecessary emails.

SCAN ME

REFERENCE LIST

Chapter 1

Brown, B. (2018, May 24). *The Midlife Unraveling—Brené Brown.*
https://brenebrown.com/articles/2018/05/24/the-midlife-unraveling/

Strenger, C., & Ruttenberg, A. (2008, February 1). The Existential
Necessity of Midlife Change. *Harvard Business Review.*
https://hbr.org/2008/02/the-existential-necessity-of-midlife-change

Chapter 2

Leisman, G., Braun-Benjamin, O., & Melillo, R. (2014). Cognitive-
motor interactions of the basal ganglia in development. *Frontiers in
Systems Neuroscience, 8.*
https://www.frontiersin.org/articles/10.3389/fnsys.2014.00016

Martins, J. (2024, February 3). *Set—And achieve—SMART-er goals.*
Asana. https://asana.com/resources/smart-goals

Chapter 3

Becker, K., Steinberg, H., & Kluge, M. (2016). Emil Kraepelin's
concepts of the phenomenology and physiology of sleep: The first
systematic description of chronotypes. *Sleep Medicine Reviews, 27,* 9–19.
https://doi.org/10.1016/j.smrv.2015.06.001

Facer-Childs, E. R., Boiling, S., & Balanos, G. M. (2018). The effects
of time of day and chronotype on cognitive and physical performance
in healthy volunteers. *Sports Medicine - Open, 4*(1), 47.
https://doi.org/10.1186/s40798-018-0162-z

Karr, J. E., Areshenkoff, C. N., Rast, P., Hofer, S. M., Iverson, G.
L., & Garcia-Barrera, M. A. (2018). The unity and diversity of executive
functions: A systematic review and re-analysis of latent variable studies.
Psychological Bulletin, 144(11), 1147–1185.
https://doi.org/10.1037/bul0000160

Leisman, G., Braun-Benjamin, O., & Melillo, R. (2014). Cognitive-motor interactions of the basal ganglia in development. *Frontiers in Systems Neuroscience, 8.* https://www.frontiersin.org/articles/10.3389/fnsys.2014.00016

Madore, K. P., & Wagner, A. D. (2019). Multicosts of Multitasking. *Cerebrum: The Dana Forum on Brain Science, 2019,* cer-04-19. https://www.ncbi.nlm.nih.gov/pmc/articles/PMC7075496/

Schoedel, R., Pargent, F., Au, Q., Völkel, S. T., Schuwerk, T., Bühner, M., & Stachl, C. (2020). To Challenge the Morning Lark and the Night Owl: Using Smartphone Sensing Data to Investigate Day–Night Behaviour Patterns. *European Journal of Personality, 34*(5), 733–752. https://doi.org/10.1002/per.2258

Shimura, A., Yokoi, K., Sugiura, K., Higashi, S., & Inoue, T. (2022). On workdays, earlier sleep for morningness and later wakeup for eveningness are associated with better work productivity. *Sleep Medicine, 92,* 73–80. https://doi.org/10.1016/j.sleep.2022.03.007

Sicinski, A. (2018, January 4). A Foolproof Method to Overcome Procrastination and Achieve Your Goals. *IQ Matrix Blog.* https://blog.iqmatrix.com/overcome-procrastination

Chapter 4

Holmes, C. (2022, September 8). *"Too much free time won't make you happier," says psychologist—How many hours you really need in a day.* CNBC. https://www.cnbc.com/2022/09/08/too-much-free-time-wont-make-you-happier-says-psychologist-how-many-hours-you-really-need-in-a-day.html

Honoré, C. (2004). *In praise of slowness: How a worldwide movement is challenging the cult of speed* (1st ed). HarperSanFrancisco.

Levitin, D. (2015). *Why the modern world is bad for your brain | Neuroscience | The Guardian.* https://www.theguardian.com/science/2015/jan/18/modern-world-bad-for-brain-daniel-j-levitin-organized-mind-information-overload

Madore, K. P., & Wagner, A. D. (2019). Multicosts of Multitasking. *Cerebrum: The Dana Forum on Brain Science, 2019,* cer-04-19. https://www.ncbi.nlm.nih.gov/pmc/articles/PMC7075496/

Pareto, V., & Montesano, A. (2014). *Manual of political economy: A critical and variorum edition* (1st ed). Oxford University Press.

Tolle, E. (2001). *The power of now.* Hodder Paperback.

Chapter 5

Brynjolfsson, E., Lorin M. Hitt, H. & Hellen, K. (2011). Strength in Numbers: How Does Data-Driven Decisionmaking Affect Firm Performance? By SSRN. https://papers.ssrn.com/sol3/papers.cfm?abstract_id=1819486

Creswell J. D. (2014). Biological pathways linking mindfulness with health. In Handbook of mindfulness: Theory, research, and practice. New York, NY: Guilford Press. A more detailed theoretical and empirical review of the mindfulness stress buffering account.

Gable, P. A., & Poole, B. D. (2012). Time Flies When You're Having Approach-Motivated Fun: Effects of Motivational Intensity on Time Perception. *Psychological Science, 23*(8), 879–886. https://doi.org/10.1177/0956797611435817

Good, D. J., Lyddy, C. J., Glomb, T. M., Bono, J. E., Brown, K. W., Duffy, M. K., Baer, R. A., Brewer, J. A., & Lazar, S. W. (2016). Contemplating Mindfulness at Work: An Integrative Review. *Journal of Management, 42*(1), 114–142. https://doi.org/10.1177/0149206315617003

Liu, Y., Ma, S., Li, J., Song, X., Du, F., & Zheng, M. (2023). Factors influencing passage of time judgment in individuals' daily lives: Evidence from the experience sampling and diary methods. *Psychological Research.* https://doi.org/10.1007/s00426-023-01859-z

Marais, G., Lantheaume, S., Fiault, R., & Shankland, R. (2020). *Mindfulness-based programs improve psychological flexibility, mental health, well-being and time management in academics.* https://doi.org/10.31234/osf.io/9w4zp

Chapter 6

Avoid the "Urgency Trap" with the Eisenhower Matrix. (n.d.). Todoist. Retrieved March 19, 2024, from https://todoist.com/productivity-methods/eisenhower-matrix

Martins, J. (2024, February 3). *Set—And achieve—SMART-er goals.* Asana. https://asana.com/resources/smart-goals

Parker, G., & Scott, S. (2023, November 30). *It's beginning to look a lot like burnout. How to take care of yourself before the holidays start.* The

Conversation. http://theconversation.com/its-beginning-to-look-a-lot-like-burnout-how-to-take-care-of-yourself-before-the-holidays-start-216175

Chapter 7

Ben-Shahar, T. (2009). *The pursuit of perfect: How to stop chasing perfection and start living a richer, happier life.* McGraw-Hill.

Gómez-Jorge, F., & Díaz-Garrido, E. (2023). The relation between Self-Esteem and Productivity: An analysis in higher education institutions. *Frontiers in Psychology, 13.* https://www.frontiersin.org/articles/10.3389/fpsyg.2022.1112437

Chapter 8

Most sources were once again referred to, as we summed up our journey to fulfilling and productive time management.

Made in United States
North Haven, CT
30 October 2024